WIPING OUT THE SPOT AND IRONING OUT THE WRINKLE

WIPING OUT THE SPOT AND IRONING OUT THE WRINKLE

MARILYN SALMONSON, D. MIN

TATE PUBLISHING
AND ENTERPRISES, LLC

Published by Tate Publishing & Enterprises, LLC
127 E. Trade Center Terrace | Mustang, Oklahoma 73064 USA
1.888.361.9473 | www.tatepublishing.com

Tate Publishing is committed to excellence in the publishing industry. The company reflects the philosophy established by the founders, based on Psalm 68:11,
"The Lord gave the word and great was the company of those who published it."

Cover design by Tyler Evans
Interior design by Nathan Harmony

Published in the United States of America

ISBN: 978-1-61566-459-7
Religion: Christian Church: General
12.01.26

Acknowledgments

For the words of this book and for making it possible for them to be shared with others, I first and foremost thank God, the Holy Spirit, and Jesus our Savior.

Thank you to my knight in shinning armor, Chris, whose love is never ending and whose passion for you, Father, is unquenching.

Thank you to Christa-Lyn and Christian Michael, my wonderful children, whose love, hugs, and kisses continue to sustain me day after day as I watch them grow into the woman and man of God they will ultimately become.

Thank you to evangelist Sally F. C. for the poem "Christianity Commercialized," a wonderful example of passion and love for God and the brethren.

Thank you, evangelist Dick Reuben, for writing the foreword. Your words continue to kindle a renewed passion for touching the very heart of God through a penitent and contrite heart.

Thank you to Pastor Adelaja Sunday, Bishop T. D. Jakes, Rabbi Ira Brawer, and Pastor George Shafer for your heartfelt words of wisdom and encouragement. I am humbled by your contribution to this project.

To Mom and Dad, Norma and Elvin Fuster; plus, my second father, "Grandpa" Walter (Bob) Salmonson, Although you are in heaven, I want you to know that I miss all of you and I will always love you. I'll see you up there one day!

Special thanks to "Grandma" Gail, who continues to love me with hugs and kisses. (My second mom)

Special thanks to everyone at Tate Publishing for your incredible patience and dedication to the completion of this project.

Special thanks to Tyler Evans, my graphic designer, for designing such a beautiful cover.

I would also like to thank all those who I did not mention by name but who, with their love, prayer, and encouragement contributed to this book with prayer, fasting, and/or wonderful encouragement: my friends who have stood with me through trials and who continue to join me celebrating in the victories in my life. They helped to make this project a reality.

Table of Contents

Foreword

Having read this manuscript, I deem it a highly explosive and a revealing exposé concerning the condition of the socialized, Sunday morning, seeker-sensitive church.

This writing is for the very mature who have the ability or skill to "chew up the apple and spit out the seeds," if there are any. This is a book that requires an honest report of self-intent and soul-searching. Let us never be so quick to be offended that we "throw the baby out with the bathwater."

I pray that this writing can get us back on the narrow path that leads to the abundant Christian life. Wide is the church road full of the theological potholes that lead to denominational bondage or legalism. I believe this is the hour of new beginnings for the church's triumph in restoring the voice of the leading of the Holy Spirit.

These are simple thoughts on restoration and healing for the church. Physical healing and restoration are a by-product of the true spiritual restoration and healing of the believer. Spiritual restoration and healing are vital elements for the future continuance of the glorious church.

Wiping out the Spot and Ironing out the Wrinkle is a clarion call to awaken the church. The old Christian hymn was not called "Backward Christian Soldier" but "Onward Christian Soldier." May the unmotivated now become the motivated! When Jesus returns, will he find you at the helm of the ship of your life, holding to a straight course of the compass of the Word of God? Remember that you are in control of sailing your own ship to its heavenly port of destiny.

—Dr. Dick Rueben, international evangelist, president, Dick Rueben Ministries Intl

Poem by Evangelist Sally F. C.
Copyright 2009
The Commercialization of Christianity

Away with the lies!
It's time to get back to the "basics"...
What happened to love, grace, and mercy?
When the prodigals came home and the pastors were
pleased and not lazy; when disciples were made and the
term *member* was used but for worldly club parties.

Christianity has been so commercialized!
In the name of mega churches.
It's too crazy; TV cameras, merchandising,
memberships, golf, bowling.
What happened to evangelizing? Don't get me wrong;
everything if done with balance can bring forth a harvest!
No one's trying to take your fun and
fame, just your fraternizing...
No one's trying to take away, your weekend
"holiday." Just shedding some light on your
addictions, making room for God's conviction...
Not just forming another tradition...
It's time to make God more than just a modern-
day fad or going to church four times a year...
Oh no, it's gonna take more than that!

Christianity has been so commercialized!

All in the name of quantity instead of
quality; religion instead of relationship;
Celebrity instead of humility;
prosperity instead of priority…
It's time to get back to the principle of the facts!
The Spirit of God is more than that!
Where is the love? Do you remember that?
Ahhh… the bliss of "first love!"
Remember when church time didn't seem long,
when we were the first to arrive and the last
to leave, still humming the "gospel" song?

Christianity has been so commercialized!

The church has imitated the world
so well. It's so hard to tell
who's going to heaven and who's going to hell!
It's time to get back to "basics" when vows were
kept and eternal life meant more than hunting
down a Christian husband or a wife, more than
looking forward to a mansion in the sky…
What happened to mercy and grace, when these
words meant something more than just a name?
What happened to the days when we could hold
our head up high (with no condemnation), bring
our sin to the throne of grace, and know that
"brethren" could be trusted with our shame?

Christianity has been so commercialized!

What would Jesus do if he walked in on you on your
highest "holy day?" Would it just be commercialized?
Like Christmas "holiday?" Would Jesus overturn
the tables in protest of our pious prosperity?
What would Jesus say at the merchandising of
his name, at the prophet pimp behind the pulpit
peddling a prophecy, like a witch (Balaam) selling
a fortune ... Lying to God's people, embezzling
by the thousands ... Miracles "for sale!"
Anointing oils with flavor, being sold
like cocktails. Oh, yeah ...

Christianity has been so commercialized!

It's time! It's time! Time to get right! No time, end
times, time for a real fight, no more commercializing,
no more merchandising, no more fraternizing,
no singles to mingle 'cause they're married to Jesus ...
No more getting paid for your singing. No more
selling, of your praising, no more tables overturning.
Bring back grace. Bring back mercy. Bring back
God's love ... Bring back the Spirit of God
descending like a dove. Bring back the days of ol'
when what mattered most was the salvation of the soul!
Bring back *repentance*!
No more commercializing Christianity.
It's time for "the basics." It's what the world
truly needs, to know the reason why Jesus
died and was buried like a seed.

To know that in knowing him, there
is satisfaction guaranteed.
To know the bottom line, that grace is not for greed,
That Jesus is the answer to everything you need!

Introduction

Wiping out the Spot and Ironing out the Wrinkle is for all who consider themselves a part of the body of Christ. This project is especially directed to those in the congregation within leadership positions and those within the pastoral calling. It identifies with the present condition of the church as a whole. It is a wake-up call for all.

Now, whether you are in leadership or not, answer this question: *Have you been hurt in the body of Christ by someone at one point or another in your life?* If the answer is yes, then this book is for you! It will shed great wisdom (from him) in promoting healing and restoration in your life.

You may have asked yourself, *How can this occur in the church?* The answer will surprise you! There are specific reasons to blame, unbeknownst to you and me. It had very little to do with the church at large. This book will reveal the reasons and will also serve you greatly in preventing you from finding yourself in a similar situation in the future.

Some today, in the body of Christ have become tolerant of one another's Christian failures and as a result have often found themselves hurting others in the process. Sadly, these have become judgmental and prideful, with no expression of love for those seeking refuge and safety within the confines of our churches.

Even though there are many who have taken great strides in addressing this problem in their ministries, there are still some whose attempts to improve their conditions have proven to be futile at times. Why? Because they have sidestepped their responsibility in the maintenance of their garment.

Make no mistake about it, the condition of our bridal garment is our responsibility. It is important not to allow our dress to become spotted and wrinkled, in poor condition for meeting our long-awaited bridegroom. Nor can we become so complacent as to cast a blind eye to the condition of our garment by evading the adjustments needed to wipe the stain of pride and iron out the wrinkle of no love on our dress.

This is why it is important not to stray from the proven norms of Christianity, (found in his Word) because when we do, we expose ourselves to the common generational dilemmas found in adopting contemporary conditional views to Christianity. These views can often leave us spiritually bankrupt, with little fruit to show for our efforts as a result.

Ideally, it is imperative that we find ourselves in the very center of the basics of Scripture (the security afforded by him) in the maintenance of our dress. Why? The holy Scriptures have always had the ability to eliminate the barriers of social economic stigmas, social physiological deficiencies, and even the technical advances of each generation.

Today, it continues to meet the needs of restoration and reconciliation in the believer! This power has been the unchanging force in shifting and molding the body of Christ. The Scriptures! They have done and continue to develop, motivate, and promote spiritual reinforcements for past, present, and future generations!

Vital to our existence, we can never forget its influence, the changing, transcending, and transforming power available to us in the simplicity of the Word of God!

Its simple truth of attaining a personal relationship with God through the manifested power of Christ by means of the sacrifice he performed on the cross is unsurpassed. It is because of this act that he established the eternal bond between man and God as a vehicle for guaranteed victory in and through our daily lives eternally!

In the following chapters, I will attempt to expose and analyze some of the misconceptions that contribute to the condition of our bridal garment, such as the difference between God's righteousness and man's righteousness and the difference between conviction and condemnation. Plus, I'll promote strategies for combating the shortcomings associated with Christian conditional behavior, which has often misguided the bride of Christ in her contemporary approach to healing, restoration, and conflict management. Also, remedies are introduced with proper applications from the foundational truths of Scripture to ensure victorious outcomes through peaceful solutions.

I have also included a chapter entitled "Pastors Only" for those specifically in leadership. It will assist with encouragement and guidance in unveiling the truths of the basic applications of the scriptures for promoting a strong, effective, and compassionate approach to ministering.

You will also find the testimonies of five successful ministers who share their key healing and restoring properties for aiding the lost and equipping the saints, all for promoting awareness for a spot-free, wrinkle-free bridal status.

Lastly, I will expose the culprit that cloaks itself within the confines of our churches, responsible for dissension and strife, and provide solutions for its demise.

In conclusion, it is my desire for those who read this project to reap a blessing and experience the urgency to return to the basics of Scripture in order to reap the great harvest of souls, for it will prove to be our greatest achievement, saved souls!

Note: If you come away from reading this project able to glean at least one golden nugget from its pages, then I rejoice! For I have accomplished his mission in the completion of this book.

Send me your testimony. I would love to hear from you. You can e-mail me at: *msalmonson@encouragingthoughts.org*.

To God always and forever will be all the glory, honor, and praise!

We Are God's Righteousness

As the bride of Christ, you and I have an obligation to identify with our righteous status, one that is honored with purity and privileged as heirs through his gift of redemption, thereby being reconciled to him in love. Our bridegroom has paid the price of our engagement and commits us to oblige. Would you agree that at times, in our zealousness to please him, we (the body of Christ) have often lost sight of our righteous identity in our quest to find and adorn our dress with added embellishments of purity and honor? On our journey, we have experimented with man-made theories, concepts, and ideals and have often fallen victim to the paradox between the traditional ritualistic righteousness of man and God's given righteousness attained through Christ Jesus, our Messiah (found in salvation). It is important to note that these (man-made) ritualistic systems of maintaining purity, consecration, sanctification, and justification have time and again held us captive to the legalism of righteous works found in religion.

Some in ministry have conceptualized the preordained traditions and standards of God by adopting and incorporating new methods of accountability where it applies to a righteous Christian walk. An example would be people who adopt methods of what I call righteous atonements, such as the wearing of specific clothing in the hopes of attaining and therefore portraying precious jewels of righteousness in their lives. This approach to righteousness has, as a result, caused God's redeeming power to restore, transition, and justify (as revealed through our Lord and Savior Jesus Christ), to be stifled at times because of the multifaceted theological views of righteousness that some believe.

As the bride of Christ, we have an obligation to identify with our righteous status.

It is important to remember that when God looks at you in Christ, he sees not only an improvement but also perfection, for God sees only his own righteousness—Jesus Christ! When Christ's righteousness is reckoned as yours, it is called justification; you are counted just (righteous) before God.

> The just shall live by faith; no one is counted just because of works, but rather by believing in Christ. It frees the believer from the idea that people are saved by works, but rather affords us the ability to live a life of faith and liberty in Christ. Not only are we saved by faith but we must also live by faith trusting in Christ.[1]

Today, we can rectify the misconceptions between self-acquired righteousness and the gifted position of right standing with God through Christ. We can reverse these misconceptions with proper attention paid to the Scriptures in identifying with who we are, taking ownership of his promises found in his simplistic message of salvation. In so doing, we promote a healthy, well-rounded, modern-day body of Christ that is governed by God's ability to restore us into a position of righteous.

F. F. Bruce puts it this way:

> But now a new way to acceptance with God has been opened up, a completely different way from that of legal obedience. Yet this is no new-fangled way thought up by us, it has ample witness borne to it in advance in the Old Testament writings—in the Law and the Prophets. It is the way of faith in Jesus Christ, and it lies open to all who believe in him, Jews and Gentiles alike. But by this new way we can be brought into a right relationship with God, and have the assurance of acceptance by him and receive his free pardon. We receive it freely, by his sheer grace, because of the redemptive work accomplished by Christ. What Christ has thus procured for us we can make effectively our own by faith. This, then, is the way in which God has demonstrated his righteousness—he has vindicated his own character and at the same time he bestows a righteous status on sinners.[2]

You and I received the righteousness of Jesus at the time of salvation. From that moment forward, we were given a fresh start as born-again believers. Jesus bestowed his robe of righteousness (as I refer to his righteousness) upon us forever. It is ours for an eternity, as stated in Romans 3:22: "Namely, the righteousness of God which comes by believing with personal trust and confident reliance on Jesus Christ (the Messiah). [And it is meant] for all who believe; for there is no distinction" (AMP).

Now that we have defined God's righteousness, do you believe *holiness* and *God's righteousness* mean the same thing? The truth is, the two terms are vastly different! I'm sure that within your circle of Christian associations you have heard the words *holiness* and *God's righteousness* in the same sentence. And yes, many believe these two terms mean the same thing, but the term *holiness* in Greek means to be *set apart*. Leviticus 11:44 says, "For I am the Lord your God. You shall therefore consecrate yourselves, and you shall be holy; for I am holy" (NKJV).

God's righteousness, on the other hand, makes you and me pure. Holiness is a process where God's righteousness is immediately transferred to you and me when we accept Christ as our Lord and Savior.

Do not confuse holiness with righteousness!

Now, let's define God's righteousness and man's righteousness.

God's Righteousness

God's Righteousness: *Dikaiosune* in Greek means *an ideal standard.*[3]

This righteousness is unattainable by obedience to any law, or by any merit of man's own, or any other condition than that of faith in Christ…The man who trusts in Christ becomes the righteousness of God in him—in Christ all that God requires a man to be, all that he could never be in himself.[4]

Man's Righteousness

(Man's) Righteousness:

> a person; just, up right, virtuous; guiltless, sinless; conforming to the precepts of divine law or accepted standards of morality; acting rightly or justly; characterized by justice or uprightness; morally right or justifiable; rightful, lawful, legitimate, rare genuine; fine, excellent; of good quality; of the preferred type.[5]

Isn't it wonderful that God's righteousness is gifted and not attained?

We are his chosen bride. Can you see yourself as God sees you? There are many benefits he has given us through his righteousness!

Therefore, you can make every effort not to confuse God-given righteousness, which is upon us, with man's acquired righteousness found in the bounding righteous works of religion (to validate our bridal status). Why?

Because our bridal dress fits perfectly! Let's relent in our quest to add additional forms of righteous adornments and adjustments to add to its beauty; instead, let's take time to examine its many benefits we stand to experience in this positional authority by making the choice to wear it correctly in our lives.

> **You and I received the righteousness of Jesus at the time of salvation.**

What Are the Benefits of God's Righteousness?

Salvation is the doorway that leads mankind into victory because of the unmerited gift of God's righteousness bestowed by him to you and me. His righteousness makes you and me pure (as we learned in the previous chapter). Man's righteousness is predicated on works, such as having qualifications met. Plus, it devises ritualistic, pompous ploys to hold the believer hostage to the many clutches of religion. Do not be fooled! You are righteous! Do not confuse living a life of rightness before him through your obedience to his commandments and statutes with that of religious statutes and qualifying stigmas enforced by contemporary theology of religion. Nothing you do outside your body will make you any more righteous before God.

God's righteousness makes you and me pure.

Did you know that the benefits of God's righteousness are transferred by and through the Holy Spirit immediately to you (the believer) at the point of accepting Jesus Christ as Lord and Savior? So, what are the benefits? Well, suddenly you are positioned into right standing with him (Jesus Christ), and he allows the Holy Spirit to take residence in us.

The Holy Spirit is powerful! He causes the positive changes in your life. He begins his work in and through you from inside out. As soon as you come to terms with your responsibility as a believer, you begin to understand the process of change in you. Holiness in our lives is a process. It is a gradual conversion that takes place in our hearts and causes us to identify the following:

1. Who dwells in us
2. An awareness of the responsibility of the position we have been given through salvation and what it represents to others
3. Who we are in Christ as believers
4. An understanding that he is holy
5. His manifested power now flowing in and through us for the working of signs, wonders, and miracles
6. That we are now the temples of the Holy Spirit

Now let's explore the benefits of accepting Jesus Christ as the Lord of your life.

1. He Dwells in You!

He is the glory of God in the manifested form of his power. When the Holy Spirit dwells in you, you have the manifested power of God in you.

> And if the Spirit of him Who raised up Jesus from the dead dwells in you, [then] he Who raised up Christ Jesus from the dead will also restore to life your mortal (short-lived, perishable) bodies through his Spirit Who dwells in you. (AMP)

The Holy Spirit never misunderstands the Father's will for your life. The Father has a purpose to work out through your life. In order that you not miss it, he places his Spirit in you. The Spirit's job is to guide you according to the will of the Father. Then the Spirit enables you to do God's will.[6]

2. He Testifies to Your Spirit and Assures You That You Are God's Child.

Romans 8:16: "The Spirit Himself [thus] testifies together with our own spirit, [assuring us] that we are children of God" (AMP).

He helps you and comforts you in your time of weakness.

How does he do this? By causing us to pray in his divine language. This type of prayer is to strengthen us and refresh us in our quest to being all that God wants us to be.

Romans 8:26–27 says:

> So too the Spirit comes to our aid and bears us up in our weakness; for we do not know what prayer to offer nor how to offer it worthily as we ought, but the Spirit Himself goes to meet our supplication and pleads in our behalf with unspeakable yearnings and groanings too deep for utterance.[7]

He knows the intent of your heart and mind and intercedes before God on your behalf. "And he Who searches the hearts of men knows what is in the mind of the Spirit [what His intent is], because the Spirit intercedes and pleads (before God) on behalf of the saints according to and in harmony with God's will" (Romans 8:27, AMP).

> Intercession of the Spirit … not only is the indwelling Spirit our pledge of Resurrection and Future Glory, but through his prayers in our behalf we are assured that God will make everything that might happen to us work together for our good. We may forget to pray. The Spirit never does. God will see us through. Let us never forget to trust him.[8]

3. He Also Requires You to Live by Faith

Romans 4:5 says, "Faith is credited to him as righteousness" (AMP).

By now, you know the benefits of his righteousness, and you have learned the difference between holiness and God's righteousness. So what's next? Now it is time to come to terms with who you are in Christ. This is important because this acknowledgment of who he is in you carries with it his authority in you!

The moment we accept Jesus as Lord in our lives, our status changes. His Word says that we are a new creation in him.

4. We Are a New Creation!

Ephesians 4:22 says, "And put on the new nature (the regenerate self) created in God's image, [Godlike] in true righteousness and holiness" (AMP). We are no longer condemned by the disobedience of Adam as a sinner but made righteous by the obedience of Christ, the righteous one.

> In other words, Jesus embodies the truth and that if (we) they wish to live in it (we) they need to put off (our) their former life and embrace one like his. The 'old man' to be put off is Adam and the 'new man,' to be put on is Christ.[9]

5. We Are in Right Standing with God!

Romans 5:18 says, "By one man we were condemned to sin and death and by one man's (Jesus) act of Righteousness we are acquitted, and we are in right standing with God" (AMP).

> Then the Son of God says, 'Yes, I am here to represent these (prisoners to sin). It is true that they are guilty, but I bore their guilt on the cross. I died in their place that they might go free. I am their righteousness.' And the judge sets them free.[10]

6. Our Sins Are All Blotted Out!

Isaiah 44:22 says, "I have blotted out like a thick cloud your transgressions, and like a cloud your sins. Return to Me, for I have redeemed you" (NKJV).

7. We Are Justified!

Romans 3:24 says, "All are justified and made upright and in right standing with God, freely and gratuitously by his grace (his unmerited favor and mercy), through the redemption which is (provided) in Christ Jesus" (AMP).

> This is a free gift, "which states that believers are justified by his (God's) grace as a gift, captures a great deal of Pauline theology in a few words. Quintessentially for Paul, justification is a gift, not a reward. It originates in God's mind, is motivated by God's character, and is purchased by God's work in Christ. It is neither human invention nor human achievement; hence, it is gracious and unmerited obviously, it occasions no opportunity for human boasting."[11]

Therefore, all are justified! Romans 5:1 says: "Therefore, since we are justified (acquitted, declared righteous, and given a right standing with God) through faith, let us (grasp the fact that we) have (the peace of reconciliation to hold and to enjoy) [have or hold on to] peace with God through our Lord Jesus" (AMP).

8. We Are Sanctified!

Romans 6:18 says, "And having been set free from sin, you have become the servants of righteousness (of conformity to the divine will in through, purpose, and action)" (AMP).

Note: "The method of positional sanctification by union with Christ; overcoming the lower 'law of sin and death,' producing righteousness and life."[12]

9. We Are Set Free From Sin!

Romans 5:18 says, "Well then, as one man's trespass [one man's false step and falling away led] to condemnation for all men, so one Man's act of righteousness (leads) to acquittal and right standing with God and life for all men" (AMP).

Sin can no longer have dominion over us!

Romans 6:14 says, "For sin shall not (any longer) exert dominion over you, since now you arc not under Law {as slaves}, but under grace (as subjects of God's favor and mercy" (AMP).

Powerful, isn't it, to experience so many wonderful benefits? However, we are required to maintain its condition of purity in our lives by obeying his law and statutes. We are to be holy. Ephesians 4:24 says, "And put on the nature (the regenerate self) created in God's image, [Godlike] in true righteousness and holiness" (AMP).

The righteousness of God demands but gives to man. We are not excused from how we choose to live our lives. From the very point that we asked Jesus into our heart, we were made righteous by his covering and are held accountable for every word and action we say and make.

Galatians 5:24–25 says, "And those who belong to Christ Jesus (the Messiah) have crucified the flesh (the godless human nature) with its passions and appetites and desire. If we live by the (Holy) Spirit, let us also walk by the Spirit. (If by the Holy Spirit we have our life in God, let us go forward walking in line, our conduct controlled by the Spirit" (AMP).

Learn to live in righteousness! Understand your position in Christ. God's righteousness brings with it all that you have need of to be successful in this life. It is a covering that embraces you from inside out. It is a position he places you in and transitions you into—a right standing with him.

> **The righteousness of God demands but gives to man.**

Your obedience to his statutes and commandments is rewarded with promises and blessings such as the promises and blessings of Abraham; the gifts of the Spirit and the fruit of the Spirit are ours!

10. The Promises and Blessings

Galatians 3:16–18 says:

> Now to Abraham and his Seed were the promises made. He does not say, "And to seeds," as of many, but as of one, "And to your Seed," who is Christ. And this I say, that the law, which was four hundred and thirty years later, cannot annul the covenant that was confirmed before by God in Christ,

that it should make the promise of no effect. For if the inheritance is of the law, it is no longer of promise; but God gave it to Abraham by promise.

NKJV

The promises of Abraham are yours!

Deuteronomy 28:1–13 says:

If you fully obey the Lord your God and carefully follow all his commands I give you today. The Lord your God will set you high above all the nations on earth. All these blessings will come upon you and accompany you if you obey the Lord your God:

You will be blessed in the city and blessed in the country. The fruit of your womb will be blessed, and the crops of your land and the young of your livestock—the calves of your herds and the lambs of your flocks. Your basket and your kneading trough will be blessed. You will be blessed when you come in and blessed when you go out. The Lord will grant that the enemies who rise up against you will be defeated before you. They will come at you from one direction but flee from you in seven. The Lord will send a blessing on your barns and on everything you put your hand to. The Lord your God will bless you in the land he is giving you. The Lord will establish you as his holy people, as he promised you on oath, if you keep the commands of the Lord your God and walk in his ways. Then all the peoples on earth will see that you are called by the name of the Lord, and they will fear you. The Lord will grant you abundant prosperity—in the fruit of your womb, the young of your livestock and the crops of your ground—in the land he swore to your forefathers to give you. The Lord will open the heavens, the storehouse of his bounty, to send rain on your land in season and to bless all the work of your hands. You will lend to many nations but will borrow from none. The Lord will make you the head, not the tail.

NIV

Galatians 3:22 says, "But the Scripture has confined all under sin, that the promise by faith in Jesus Christ might be given to those who believe" (NKJV).

Galatians 3:26–29 also says:

You are all sons of God through faith in Christ Jesus, for all of you who were baptized into Christ have clothed yourselves with Christ. There is neither Jew nor Greek, slave nor free, male nor female, for you are all one in Christ Jesus. If you belong to Christ, then you are Abraham's seed, and heirs according to the promise.

NIV

11. The Gifts of the Holy Spirit

First Corinthians 12:1–11 says:

Now concerning spiritual gifts, brethren, I do not want you to be ignorant: You know that you were Gentiles, carried away to these dumb idols, however you were led. Therefore I make known to you that no one speaking by the Spirit of God calls Jesus accursed, and no one can say that Jesus is

> Lord except by the Holy Spirit. There are diversities of gifts, but the same Spirit. There are differences of ministries, but the same Lord. And there are diversities of activities, but it is the same God who works all in all. But the manifestation of the Spirit is given to each one for the profit of all: for to one is given the word of wisdom through the Spirit, to another the word of knowledge through the same Spirit, to another faith by the same Spirit, to another gifts of healings by the same Spirit, to another the working of miracles, to another prophecy, to another discerning of spirits, to another different kinds of tongues, to another the interpretation of tongues. But one and the same Spirit works all these things, distributing to each one individually as he wills.
>
> NKJV

The gifts of the Holy Spirit are yours!

The gifts of the Spirit were expounded upon by Dr. Lester Sumrall. His study revealed the following about the gifts. According to Dr. Sumrall, there are nine gifts, divided into three categories: the revelation gifts, the power gifts, and the inspiring gifts.

The revelation gifts include:

1. The Word of Wisdom–is a revelation of the prophetic future under the anointing of God. It deals with future revelations.
2. The Word of Knowledge–is the revealing of a fact in

existence which can only be supernaturally revealed. It deals with facts that exist in the present.

3. The Discerning of Spirits–this deals with the comprehending of the human spirit, supernaturally revealed by the Holy Spirit, both good and bad.

The power gifts include:

1. The Gift of Faith–this gift of faith is different from other types of faith. It is a special faith that supernaturally achieves what is impossible through human instruments. This gift deals with God bringing to pass a supernatural change. (No human effort is involved in accomplishing the change.)
2. The Working of Miracles Gift–deals with the works through a human instrument, a person who does a supernatural act by the divine energy of the Holy Spirit, such as the man in the Bible called Samson, who killed the lion with his bare hands. Judges 14:6 says, "The Spirit of the Lord came upon him in power so that he tore the lion apart with his bare hands as he might have torn a young goat" (NIV).
3. The Gifts of Healing–this gift is the only gift of the nine that is in the plural form. (It deals with more than one aspect of healing.) God uses a person by the Holy Spirit to pray for a particular kind of sickness or disease. (Keep in mind that there might be as many gifts of healing as there are diseases. This is why the term is plural.)

The inspirational gifts include:

Note: God brings his anointing and his blessing to the church. Now, usually these gifts have to do with a corporate setting.

1. Gift of Prophecy–a person, through the unction of the Holy Spirit, speaks forth words of edification, exhortation, and comfort; words supernaturally given to the church from God.
2. Gift of Unknown Tongues–this is a ministry of proclaiming in a public meeting a message from God in a language not understood by the person giving it. Then the gift of interpretation of tongues goes into operation.
3. Gift of Interpretation of Tongues–this gift is used without any mental faculties being involved; the message that has been given in another language is supernaturally interpreted by the Holy Spirit through another."[13]

12. The Fruit of the Holy Spirit

Galatians 5:22–23 says, "But the fruit of the Spirit is love, joy, peace, longsuffering, kindness, goodness, faithfulness, gentleness, self-control. Against such there is no law" (NKJV). The fruit of the Holy Spirit is yours! The fruit of the Holy Spirit is available to you also because he dwells in you.

What is the fruit of the Holy Spirit?

- Love
- Joy

- Peace
- Longsuffering
- Kindness
- Goodness
- Faithfulness
- Gentleness
- Self-Control

Therefore he is able to afford us the privilege of making these character enhancements (as I like to call them) available to us. These are called fruit for a reason. I believe it is because as we continue on our journey of faith, the fruit ripens! It becomes sweet-tasting to those experiencing the benefits of the fruit in the believer as they behave accordingly in their daily Christian living and witness.

The fruit is given to us for the purpose of multiplying it. The harvest of the fruit we possess is in others. How? I believe as the fruit ripens within us, it becomes a sweet savor for our Heavenly Father as well, and he uses its harvest in us to multiply its seeds (of kindness, gentleness, etc.) in others.

How? Because the seeds we sow will always reproduce after its kind to those who encounter us and those who are encountered by them (the ones who cross their path). This is accomplished all for the express purpose that they may partake of its harvest and be drawn to the facilitator of those seeds, God himself.

All of these promises, blessings, gifts, and fruit are

yours as his bride and his heir. You must exercise your authority! Today, imagine his righteousness upon you!

His righteousness also provides safety! His righteousness is an offensive weapon that protects you from the enemy! It never loses its effectiveness against the enemy's plan for your life. However, if you do not wear his righteousness correctly, it is of little value in protecting you. Its effectiveness in protecting you and I is predicated on how we choose to wear it. Too many of us are walking around with his righteousness unbuttoned, unfastened, partially on, or with only one arm in one of the sleeves and the rest of it dragging behind us because of un-confessed sin in our lives.

Satan loves it when we allow ourselves to get complacent in our wearing of the dress. It happens so gradually. The moment you commit a sin, its buttons begin to unfasten, one button at a time. If you do not repent and continue to commit yet another sin on top of the one committed beforehand, you commence on a road of sin without repenting, and this triggers added buttons on your dress to unfasten. Soon, if you are not careful to repent, you will find yourself living a life that only displays defeat "like a man walking down a street with his head bowed over in a slumped position, dragging part of his 'coat or robe' behind him. It is cold and rainy out side, and he struggles to get to where he is going because he is exposed to the elements of the weather."[14]

Unfortunately, because the body of the person in this example is exposed and vulnerable to the brutal weather of the day, he is a poor portrait of the victories in his life. Notice the responsibility of repentance and utilizing it as a tool for allowing him to readjust your dress (refasten its buttons) is yours!

Our obedience to him protects us from the elements of the enemy's strategic warfare. It is in our obedience to him that he commands blessings and victory in and through our lives.

Today, imagine his righteousness upon you!

We (the body of Christ) are required for such a time as this to walk by the Spirit more than ever! It is almost as if the teachings and knowledge of his Word have made a demand on our daily lives. When we walk by his Spirit, allowing him to lead our every step, our future is visible. It is for this reason that we must rise up and understand his authority in our lives.

He is calling us to attention! We cannot allow ourselves to sit in a blemished dress due to misconceptions and disillusions, declaring righteousness by works conditional to ritualistic traditions and pious, self-imposed contemporary theological laws and regulations. We can, however, strive for mastery in maintaining a "bride status" on a daily basis in our determination to succeed by defeating the entanglement of misinterpretations of the Bible in our desire to serve God with all our hearts, minds, and spirits and living our lives guided by the godly principles set forth in his commandments and statutes ordained in his Word.

Our bridal garment can radiate with brilliance, beauty, and purity as we prepare for the bridegroom to come. It can be free from spot and wrinkle for our meeting! Ephesians

5:27 states, "That he might present it to himself a glorious church, not having spot, or wrinkle, or any such thing; but that it should be holy and without blemish" (KJV).

When we walk by his Spirit, allowing him to lead our every step, our future is visible.

Identifying Christian Conditional Behavior

In the previous chapter, we learned the importance of understanding the difference between self-righteousness and his righteousness, what the benefits of his righteousness are, who we are in Christ, etc., plus the validity of fully embracing their knowledge for promoting victory in our lives! Now, in order to fully come to terms with whose we are, we must undoubtedly identify: (a) sin, (b) what I call Christian Conditional Behavior (CCB), and (c) what these two terms have in common with each other and how they affect you and me. I understand that this is a new term. It was given to me by the Lord. I will define this term a little later.

Let's define sin according to the scriptures in order to appreciate the victory of overcoming sin. So what is sin? Sin is rebellion against God (by God's standards), according to Genesis 39:9b: "How then can I do this great wickedness, and sin against God?" (NKJV) Psalm 51:4 says,

"Against You, You only, have I sinned, And done this evil in Your sight—That You may be found just when You speak, And blameless when You judge." (NKJV) Romans 3:23 says, "For all have sinned and fall short of the glory of God." (NKJV).

As believers, it is necessary to come to terms with the sin in our lives so it can be properly communicated from the pulpit in a convicting fashion, not a condemning one. Why? To cause repentance in the hearer.

In order to define sin in our lives, it is important to address the emotional state of our humanity then use it as an avenue to evangelize the truths of embracing total healing—mind, spirit, emotion, and body through who dwells in us. Why? Because if we do not separate the emotions, mind, and body from the spirit, we render healing and restoration subject to our feelings and intellect instead of embracing healing and restoration by faith. If we choose to ignore this vital truth, we will continue to look at the past failures of sin in order to identify with who we are instead of whose we are.

I know that we have not been taught that the wounds of our emotions are a vital part of how we perceive ourselves as believers, but they are present in the fibers of our mind and heart. Therefore, they are a vital part of our body, which helps us to calculate and assimilate God's wisdom, necessary to avoid the future nets of enticements frequently set before us by the enemy. It is in our acknowledgement that these wounds exist that we activate God's healing power by our simple attempt to obey his standards. It is this action of obedience in sidestepping those nets laid by the enemy to cause us to stumble that we triumph over them!

It is important to properly define sin and its effects from the pulpit.

How do we address sin from the pulpit?

Several years ago, after I addressed a church congregation, I began to exit the church. As I reached the parking lot, God arrested me in the spirit. He said, *Marilyn, tell them what they are doing right, and let me tell them what they are doing wrong.* Needless to say, I was completely overwhelmed with a sense of sorrow, for he had given me this opportunity to address others in the body, and I had failed to do it his way. Unknowingly, in my zeal to serve his cause, I had communicated condemnation from the pulpit instead encouragement for them to continue to overcome. I immediately repented and asked the Lord to fulfill his purpose in my life. Since then, I have purposed in my heart to always allow the Holy Spirit to do the convicting.

Does this experience bear witness in you? As a leader, where do you find yourself today? Are you remedying sin with conviction or condemnation?

For many of us in ministry, we have "been there and done that." At times, we have also inadvertently chosen to group the emotional and spiritual repercussions of sin into a unified state of consciousness. Note the repercussions of sin to the emotions and the spirit are separate. Why? Because one is subject to the other. Our emotions are always subject to the spirit. It is important to address both the emotions and spiritual conditions of our Christian walk in order to lead productive, fruitful lives, effective for God's call on our lives. However, let's remember that the spiritual side of Whose we are will always carry conviction qualities with it. Why? (The Holy Spirit dwells in us).

These qualities always bring forth self-value as opposed to the condemning antics of our emotions, which often convey worthlessness and inadequateness in us when we sin (i.e., conviction creates salvation as a setting to free one from the bondage promoted by condemnation). Conviction deals with the issues of the spirit, whereas condemnation deals with the emotional issues that cause us to shrink back.

As a leader, where do you find yourself today? Are you remedying sin with conviction or condemnation?

We cannot fail in our presentation of sin and its effects on the body. What happens when we fail to treat these issues or address them adequately from the pulpit to those inside and outside of the in the body of Christ? For those inside the church, it promotes a distorted image of salvation and God's promises. For those in the world, their perspective of him is affected! Why? They equate us with him; we represent him. Failure to address these issues properly is often the pointed reason for our unattractiveness to the secular world. Why? Because the much-needed difference they need to see in us lies in the healing power of Christ in us. We must fulfill our purpose in our quest of reaching the lost by conveying the evidence of his power! It must be seen from the "worldly bleachers" as they peek over the walls of our sanctuaries to watch our every move!

The evidence of his power should be the captivating force drawing the secular world system to him as they journey in their quest of finding the only remedy to their spiritual and emotional deficiencies.

Remember, conviction creates salvation as a setting to free one from the bondage promoted by condemnation. Therefore, to reach the modern-day lost, we cannot afford to sever the ties to the traditional, simplistic digestion of the messages outlined in the Word. The balance and sensitivity in our assessment of the underlying crises this world is in are necessary!

Ask yourself, *Is my sanctuary a place of social boosting of self-image or a place of healing, restoration, and refuge?* Statements such as *I'm saved, I'm blessed, I'm healthy, wealthy, and wise* (heard repeatedly in many of our Christian circles) serve as a proclamation of victory! However, often these statements are uttered carelessly because of Christian Conditional Behavior, which bears witness to a forced blind eye to the failures that lie un-nurtured, undiscovered, unwarranted, and unwanted within our sanctuaries.

These types of statements, when stated in passing with no regard to the true situation surrounding the person associated with the comment, promote what I refer to as Christian Conditional Behavior. To better understand this term, let's define *conditional behavior.*

Conditional behavior can also be called *operant con-*

ditioning or *instrumental conditioning*. It is a process of changing behavior by rewarding or punishing a subject each time an action is performed until the subject associates the action with pleasure or distress.[15]

Christian Conditional Behavior (CCB), in my opinion, is similar to the definition above in that it often rewards the believer with a sense of sainthood (self-righteousness) when the believer complies with its qualifications set forth by the set of social norms within the congregational church community (Note: Not all norms are the same. Each one is unique to its Christian denomination or church). CCB can also punish the believer who does not comply or fit into its regimented social norms with labels.

In my observation, CCB forces the believer to live with bared emotions. How? It promotes an attempt to censor and confine his or her sin or sinful energies to the privacy of the believer's home. Have you heard the term, *putting on your Sunday face*? Oddly enough, the believer, in fear of being found out, becomes cautious and puts on his or her Sunday face; therefore, he/she continues to function as a normal, victorious, saved saint in front of fellow believers, to the point of even denying that a problem exists, conniving, even, at times when trying to avoid the possibilities of being labeled. What do I mean by *labeling*? The believer comes to fear his or her church brethren's labeling in what I call the back-sliding, blackballing effect with dreaded taboos like, *Oh, he or she missed it*, or, *He or she is back-sliding*."

Christian conditional behavior is man-imposed, not God's compulsion for us! It does not deal with sin and its effects! It promotes hiding, and the effects are ignored and allowed to continue to fester.

This is why it is important not to allow your church to become a place associated with CCB or allow it to become a saint membership club, which entitles one to be seen as strictly being successful (in one's own eyes), as opposed to the one who is in the process of overcoming through Christ Jesus. The world is not fooled! They can see our failures! They can often see little or no difference between our problems and theirs when we allow our churches to become social clubs instead of sanctuaries.

Conditional Christian Conditional Behavior is man imposed, not God's compulsion for the believer.

Statistics show:

- More than 70 million adults are currently struggling to find meaning and purpose in life.
- More than 25 million people are profoundly lonely, and most of them are not elderly people living alone after the death of a spouse.
- More than 50 million citizens have endured the hardship of divorce, which exacts a toll on people's lives for years after the marriage is dissolved.
- More than 20 million adults have serious problems with gambling.
- An unknown number of adults and children suffer from physical abuse, typically at the hands of family members, and while estimates of such

abusive behavior exist, they are almost certainly substantially lower than the reality.

- Substance abuse continues to plague the nation, with alcoholism on the rise and drug use stubbornly maintaining ground despite legislative and legal enforcement efforts to rid the land of illegal narcotics.
- The most frequent concern registered by teenagers and adolescents is that they do not receive unconditional love from their parents. This hardship afflicts an estimated two out of three kids in the United States between the ages of eight and eighteen.[16]

Christian Conditional Behavior in the body of Christ causes the believer to fall prey to habitual offenders who cloak themselves with church salvation only to find themselves empty as underachievers because CCB fails to identify and formulate answers to their hemorrhaging emotional and spiritual issues that are present in their lives. Why? Because CCB purposely ignores and is afraid to admit that there is a greater dimension of healing not provided in just reciting the sinner's prayer.

When we make Jesus the Lord of our lives, through faith we can experience immediate and total healing! But in some, this transition from salvation to surrendering their total lives to Christ and making him Lord of their lives takes a process of time.

Why does CCB fail to confront the emotional or physical problems that plague the church today?

1. A belief that, at the core of Christian faith, it should be more concerned about outward behavior than inner transformation.
2. An unwillingness to grant a healthy anonymity to those who are in great pain.
3. An unwillingness to network with others (such as medical organizations) to make sure hurting people get the help they need.
4. A belief that the mission of the church is to make Christians perfect rather than to keep us moving forward on the road of life in Christ (We are all pilgrims on this journey, not arrivals.)
5. A tendency to meddle in homes rather than simply being available to serve.
6. Dishonesty and unwillingness on the part of leaders to be open about their own shortcomings and failures.
7. The use of guilt as a motivator.
8. Excess church debt, which gives money, more than people, the upper hand in church decision making.
9. The discouragement or prohibitions of women from positions of leadership.
10. The overscheduling of meetings, keeping families from spending the time together they need to be healthy.

11. An unwillingness to put a stop to backbiting and gossip.
12. A tendency to major on minors, for example, abortion, politics, tongues, deliverance, while forgetting Bible training and the key issues of love, joy, and peace.
13. Immorality among leaders and unwillingness to confront immorality.
14. A tendency to remain isolated from other churches.
15. We are too self-centered to admit the crises exist in my congregation.[17]

These Christian conditional behavioral traits encourage hiding and postpone the healing process. Yes, I believe total healing, inclusive of emotions, mind, spirit, and the physical body is possible with just one touch of the Lord. However, I also believe that until the CCB is identified and rendered powerless within the four walls of our sanctuaries, it will continue to cause havoc. It is possible within the four walls to position ourselves in the place of welcoming and embracing total healing by affording ourselves and others the benefits found in sanctuary.

Sanctuary by definition means *a sacred place, such as a church, temple, or mosque; the holiest part of a sacred place, as the part of a Christian church around the altar; a church, in which fugitives are afforded immunity to arrest and punishment; Immunity to arrest afforded by a sanctuary; a place of refuge or asylum.*[18]

How do we position ourselves in the place of welcoming and embracing total healing by affording ourselves and others the benefits found in the sanctuary? How do we break the hold of CCB? We acknowledge the problem and take a stance with the remedies presented below, making a conscious effort to embrace the power of the manifestation of the Holy Spirit, which can heal and restore the totality of man, spiritually, emotionally, mentally, and physically. I dare say, we can render CCB ineffective in the churches by acknowledging its existence! Also, it is vital to acknowledge the totally of sin and its effects on man by definition and communicate these properly from the pulpit, especially to those affected by CCB. Otherwise, there will continue to be the undeniable effects of injuries incurred among believers and unbelievers alike in the church, which rob the potential of effectively bearing great fruit for the kingdom of God.

It is prudent to mention that those with CCB will remain broken, and some eventually will go AWOL if left uninformed! Why? Simply because this behavior fails to conceptualize God's unconditional love where it pertains to Scripture and fails to meet the healing requirements for restoring the injured. On the other side of the coin, those who are injured by the contributing sin factors and ailments caused by CCB will continue to thrive because CCB continues to sweep the sin factors under the rug and denies their existence.

Other contributing factors to the cause of CCB are often found in the man-made ritualistic traditions of what they perceive religion should be in picking apart the fabric of God's patterns, causing the believer to fall short of the mark, thereby holding him or her captive to CCB as a result. Consequently, it is also important to be careful with not entangling ourselves with their (those affected with CCB) misconceptions of God's Word. CCB, if left to fester, renders one invalid and unsubstantial in his or her reality and forces one to put effort into judging others. Plus, it causes one to overstep the boundaries of others. This invasion with no remedy to offer keeps one in bondage to the habitual failures of CCB. It is a cycle that can be broken by taking a hold of the truths in God's Holy Word!

> **God called us to be ambassadors. He never called us to be policemen.**
>
> **It is not our job to enforce the gospel. It is our job to present the gospel.**

Earlier, I mentioned the mark. You might be wondering, *What is the mark?* Well, the mark is the conveying of God's unconditional love and mercy to our brothers and sisters in Christ and to those who have yet to experience him.

What Are the Remedies for Obliterating Christian Conditional Behavior?

Ask yourself, *How can we render CCB powerless? What is the remedy?* The answer is called boundaries.

Listed below are several examples of the remedies. The Bible may not use the word *boundary*, but many scripture verses, when combined, give you and me helpful insight into the patterns that make for healthy boundary keeping. These boundaries are needed to promote healing and restoration. The author of *Churches That Heal*, Doug

Murren, elaborates on some of these issues. Murren says, "I call these 'one another' passages because they tell us how we are to relate to one another as brothers and sisters in Christ. I believe that when we put these passages together, a clear picture arises of a healthy and respectful church."[19]

If we analyze this list, we catch a glimpse of God's intention and plan for the role of the church.

Say this with me: "We can defeat Christian conditional behavior!"

What does God say? Let's review God's Word!

- The believers are devoted to one another and find preference to one another (Romans 12:10: "Be kindly affectionate to one another with brotherly love, in honor giving preference to one another.")
- They love one another (Romans 13:8: "Owe no one anything except to love one another, for he who loves another has fulfilled the law.")
- They refrain from judging one another (Romans 14:13: "Therefore let us not judge one another anymore, but rather resolve this, not to put a stumbling block or a cause to fall in our brother's way.")
- They edify one another (Romans 14:19: "Therefore let us pursue the things which make for peace and the things by which one may edify another.")
- They instruct one another (Romans 15:14: "Now I myself am confident concerning you, my brethren, that you also are full of goodness, filled with all knowledge, able also to admonish one another.")

- They serve one another (Galatians 5:13: "For you, brethren, have been called to liberty; only do not use liberty as an opportunity for the flesh, but through love serve one another.")
- They do not hurt one another (Galatians 5:15: "But if you bite and devour one another, beware lest you be consumed by one another!")
- They do not provoke one another through conceit (Galatians 5:26: "Let us not become conceited, provoking one another, envying one another.")
- They help carry one another's burdens (Galatians 6:2: "Bear one another's burdens, and so fulfill the law of Christ.")
- They are patient with one another (Ephesians 4:2: "With all lowliness and gentleness, with longsuffering, bearing with one another in love.")
- They are kind and forgiving toward one another (Ephesians 4:32: "And be kind to one another, tenderhearted, forgiving one another, just as God in Christ forgave you.")[20]

As I began to examine this list, my predefined, God-sided thoughts caused me to embrace these godly remedies from God's Word to put a voice to all those affected by CCB and our wounded, churched folk. Can you hear their cry? *Help me! Don't judge me! Don't hurt me! Show me love!*

Can you as a leader say, "You're safe here. Let's get you healed"?

Today, we can put into effect these powerful remedies from God's Word in order to strive to be trustworthy and create an environment of compassion, trust, and acceptance with (forgiveness) in our sanctuaries as a focus. Doing so will communicate to one another and those seeking refuge, *You're safe here. Let's get you healed.*

All for the purpose of advocating, activating, promoting, and proclaiming to the world, *we have the answers to your pain—healing and restoration through the saving knowledge and experience of Christ!*

Say this with me: *Yes, we can, for the cause of Christ, in his compassionate attitude. We can take inventory of the hurts caused by the elements of CCB!* We can pull ourselves up by our bootstraps *and make the much-needed effort to render CCB ineffective and inoperative in our sanctuaries in spite of the common threat of becoming too committed to the cause (for our own good) by relying wholeheartedly on the undiluted, living Word of God as our guide!*

Can You Hear the Clarion Call?

"Let him who has ears, let him hear!"

Awake! Awake!" Come to the aid of those infected by the deadly virus of misinterpretation, miscalculations, misconstrued revelations, and formulated theories of God's Word, works, commands, compassion, and love!

Yes, we can! We can identify with whose we are in order to truly succeed in all we do!

> **Thus says the Lord of Hosts:**
>
> **"Tear down the Altars of Judgment and begin to build Altars of Mercy for the next wave to embrace The Body of Christ will be the down-**

trodden. They will have the most to be forgiven. They will be the most grateful. They will be the most committed.

They will bring in the greatest harvest for such a time as this ..." (Spoken to my heart during prayer.)

Our bridal garment can radiate with brilliance, beauty, and purity as we prepare for the bridegroom to come. It can be free from spot and wrinkle for our meeting!

When we walk by his Spirit, allowing him to lead our every step, our future is visible.

Conflict Management

So far, we have learned a great deal about the authority we possess in Christ, plus some of the areas of opportunity in the church when dealing with the issue of healing and restoration and its effects, such as the role Christian Conditional Behavior plays in its demise.

I continue with the subject of healing and restoration by introducing you to the subject of conflict management and the reasons why conflict often takes place in the body of Christ.

A positive conflict management program is a powerful tool in dealing with the void that exists on the shelves of Christian debates within the four walls. A conflict management awareness program can ensure the survival of those involved in debates without enduring the casualties of lost relationships and injured souls as its outcome. Conflict management plays a vital role in the body of Christ by serving as an example to the secular world of his witness. It is also a great asset to the body of Christ when dealing with the conflicts that arise between the brethren.

Conflict management is a tool that utilizes a solution to a situation from the standpoint of peace. As such, it has the powerful ingredients for creating, developing, and embracing the victory without the struggle of chaos and strife. This can prove to be an extraordinary resolution to conflict, given the many confrontations, disillusions, and demises plaguing the bride of Christ in these latter times of such darkness.

As you know, the integrity and character of our bridal garment is fundamental to our witness as believers! Therefore, to find the answers one could put into action when dealing with conflict in the body of Christ, I searched for several cherished principles that offer aid to conflict management. These points settled quietly in the biblical statutes of Scriptures were shared by Apostle Paul several thousand years ago. He covered the area of conflict from two standpoints: the secular viewpoint and the biblical viewpoint.

Biblical View

First, his biblical teachings on the subject bring to light some of the reasons why we, at times, have failed in our attempts to implement peaceful solutions to conflict. He goes on to say that there are idols in our lives. Then he exposes these idols in our lives that contribute to our defeat in addressing conflict from a positive perspective. We can strive in our efforts to produce a harvest of peace instead of engaging in destroying its outcome with the judgmental, conceited, and seducing, conditional worldly behavior supported by retaliation.

Conflict is defined as *a fight, a battle, a (prolonged) struggle between opposing forces: fighting, strife; the clashing or variance of opposed principles, beliefs, etc., (the emotional distress due to) the opposition of incompatible wishes etc., in a person.*[21]

Conflict management from a biblical view is a difference in opinion or purpose that frustrates someone's goals or desires. This definition is broad enough to include innocuous (inoffensive) conflicts such as variations in taste, i.e. one spouse wanting to vacation in the mountains while the other prefers the oceans, as well as hostile arguments, such as fights, quarrels, lawsuits, or church divisions. The Bible does not teach that all conflict is bad. Instead, it teaches that some differences are natural and beneficial. Since God has created us as unique individuals, human beings will often have different opinions, convictions, desire, perspective, and priorities. Therefore, although we should seek unity in our relationships, we should not demand uniformity (Ephesians 4:1–13).[22]

Ephesians 4:1–13 says (Paul is speaking):

> I, therefore, the prisoner of the Lord, beseech you to walk worthy of the calling with which you were called, with all lowliness and gentleness, with longsuffering, bearing with one another in love, endeavoring to keep the unity of the Spirit in the bond of peace. There is one body and one Spirit, just as you were called in one hope of your calling; one Lord, one faith, one baptism; one God and Father of all, who is above all, and through

> all, and in you all. But to each one of us grace was given according to the measure of Christ's gift. Therefore he says: "When he ascended on high, he led captivity captive, And gave gifts to men." (Now this, "He ascended." What does it mean but that He also first descended into the lower parts of the earth? He who descended is also the One who ascended far above all the heavens, that He might fill all things.) And he Himself gave some to be apostles, some prophets, some evangelists, and some pastors and teachers, for the equipping of the saints for the work of ministry, for the edifying of the body of Christ, till we all come to the unity of the faith and of the knowledge of the Son of God, to a perfect man, to the measure of the stature of the fullness of Christ.
>
> NKJV

The Apostle Paul reminds us of the insightful biblical principles to combat and confront conflict:

1. Rejoice in the Lord always: Maintaining a God-centered attitude.
2. Let your gentleness be evident to all: *Gentleness* in the Greek is *epiaches*, which means forbearing, large heart, gentle, courteous, considerate, generous, lenient and/or moderate.[23] Galatians 6:1–2 says, "Brethren, if a man is overtaken in any trespass, you who are spiritual restore such a one in a spirit of gentleness, considering yourself lest you also be tempted. Bear one another's burdens, and so fulfill the law of Christ" (NKJV).

3. Replace anxiety with prayer: Anxiety is the Greek word *merimnao*, which means trivial concerns.[24] Mathew 6:25–34 says:

> Therefore I say to you, do not worry about your life, what you will eat or what you will drink; nor about your body, what you will put on. Is not life more than food and the body more than clothing? Look at the birds of the air, for they neither sow nor reap nor gather into barns; yet your heavenly Father feeds them. Are you not of more value than they? Which of you by worrying can add one cubit to his stature? So why do you worry about clothing? Consider the lilies of the field, how they grow: they neither toil nor spin; and yet I say to you that even Solomon in all his glory was not arrayed like one of these. Now if God so clothes the grass of the field, which today is, and tomorrow is thrown into the oven, will he not much more clothe you, O you of little faith? Therefore do not worry, saying, 'What shall we eat?' or 'What shall we drink?' or 'What shall we wear?' For after all these things the Gentiles seek. For your heavenly Father knows that you need all these things. But seek first the kingdom of God and his righteousness, and all these things shall be added to you. Therefore do not worry about tomorrow, for tomorrow will worry about its own things. Sufficient for the day is its own trouble.
>
> NKJV

4. Practice what you've learned.[25] Philippians 4:9 says, "The things which you learned and received and heard and saw in me, these do, and the God of peace will be with you" (NKJV). This verse speaks of applying what is shared in the Word to the problems that arise in our lives, to activate the possibilities of hope, faith, and fulfillment even at the brink of despair!

As I mentioned earlier, the Bible does not teach that all conflict is bad. Instead, it teaches that some differences are natural and beneficial. Incredibly, the ability to resolve issues at this level is explosive by world standards! God's formula is an effective, compassionate, and systematic biblical profile. It addresses underlining, nonproductive, abrasive situations that arise in ministry among the brethren. It is effective and commendable! The assimilating of God's scriptural concepts in this area is necessary, so we can strive in our efforts to produce a harvest of peace instead of engaging in destroying its outcome with a judgmental, conceited, and seducing, conditional worldly behavior supported by retaliation. It is important to remember that healing and restoring the wounded is encouraged in the eternal promise, purpose, and example shared by our one and only Savior, Jesus Christ.

Conflict Management from the Secular View

From his second biblical teaching, the Apostle Paul addresses the subject of conflict management in an area often overlooked by our churches. It is conflict management from a judicial system view or secular view. It can prove to be extremely ineffective as an alternative Christian view to conflict management. Bear in mind God's foundational statutes for dealing with controversy successfully is powerful! It can never be replaced by utilizing a judicial approach to gain the victory in any given situation you face!

You may be asking, *Why should I not look at the judicial system as a way to vindicate myself?* Put simply

> Our courts are not equipped to deal with the personal side of conflict. The adversarial process is designed to resolve legal issues, not to reconcile people or help them change the attitudes and habits that lead to conflict. In fact, lawsuits usually drive people further apart and often ingrain the beliefs and behavior that lead to controversy.[26]

The Apostle Paul addressed this in 1 Corinthians 6:1–8.

> Does any one of you, when he has a case against his neighbor, dare to go to law before the unrighteous, and not before the saints? Or do you not know that the saints will judge the world? And if the world is judged by you are you not competent to constitute the smallest law courts? Do you not know that we shall judge angels? How much more, matters of this life? If then you have law courts dealing with matters of this life, do you appoint them as judges who are of no account in the church? I say this to your shame. Is it so, that there is not among you one wise man who will be

> able to decide between his brethren, but brother goes to law with brother, and that before unbelievers? Actually, then, it is already a defeat for you, that you have lawsuits with one another. Why not rather be wronged? Why not rather be defrauded? On the contrary, you yourselves wrong and defraud, and that your brethren.
>
> NASB

The Word of God is clear. Do you see the difference between a godly and a worldly view approach to conflict management? Which one would you choose? Don't be fooled!

Failing at Peacemaking: God's Solution to Conflict!

Why do we sometimes fail in our attempt to resolve conflict from a biblical perspective? Despondently, although we (believers) have sought to wear the vesture of God's love, and carry his banner called peacemaker into our homes, our churches and our community, we often fail for several reasons, according to the book *The Peace Maker*, by Ken Sande.

What are the reasons for failure to deal with conflict from a peace standpoint?

He outlines the following:

1. The lack of examples seen in our spiritual leaders when confronted with conflict in their lives. (Often, conflict is handled behind closed doors in an attempt to defuse judgment and condemnation from those under their leadership.)

2. The lack in acknowledging the advantages and security found within the very sanctuary of brethren and the wisdom found in the application of biblical text in addressing conflict and debate. (Proverb 24:6: "For by wise counsel you will wage your own war, and in a multitude of counselors there is safety." NKJV)
3. The lack of awareness and insensitivity to the cause of Christ. "The best way to counteract this tendency is to get your eyes off yourself and to focus on God."[27] (Colossians 3:1–2: "Since, then, you have been raised with Christ, set your hearts on things above, where Christ is seated at the right hand of God. Set your minds on things above, not on earthly things." NIV).

Do these reasons sound familiar? These reasons are also attributed to Christian Conditional Behavior. Have you been affected by any of these in your church? These are manifestations of the consequences found in being infected with CCB. Can you see it? This is why a realignment of Christian standards in dealing with conflict is needed to alert us to the repercussions of conflict, in case we choose to ignore the applications of godly principles in living our lives.

Conflict management is vital to the maintenance of our bridal garment. These repercussions of conflict are generated due to CCB and are what are referred to as idols in our lives. It is important that we are wise to their existence.

Together, we (believers) can bring to light the erosion taking place in our lives due to the idols that manifest themselves in us, which try to replace and dethrone our Savior from being Lord of our lives on a daily basis. How? Simply by exposing them! How do we expose these hidden idols and defeat them? The answers are found in his Word! It is called getting back to the basics of scripture.

Let's expose them today!

Hidden Idols

We can render them inoperative and ineffective in our lives through Christ who strengthens us!

What are the hidden idols?

1. Improper desires for physical pleasure; lust of the flesh
2. Pride and arrogance; to be preoccupied with one's own wisdom, accomplishments, power, abilities, reputation, or possessions
3. Love of money (other material possessions)
4. Fear of man (fear of what others can do to us); excessive concern about what others think about us.
5. Good things that we want too much. The most difficult idols to deal with are good desires that we elevate to demands. These most subtle idols include love, happiness, good health, accomplishments, success, prosperity, recreation, goodwill, influence, status, a good image, or even spiritual power. These things, while beneficial in themselves, can become idols if we want them for the wrong reasons, if our thoughts and actions revolve around

> them, or if our failure to have them is a major source of discontent. Idols—the things of the world—can motivate or master us. They influence what we think about, where we invest our time, how we handle our rights and resources, and how we deal with other people.[28]

Beware, for the devil uses these forms of unidentified idols as strategies to entangle, estrange, and pollute the very essence of brotherhood found in brethren. His attempt to promote division, contention, and discord in the body of Christ is always prevalent in the form of idol worship!

What does the Word of God say about these idols?

1. Improper desires for physical pleasure; lust of the flesh: This kind of idol is often characterized by an aversion to disciplining one's mind, spirit, or body. Lusts of the flesh can include sexual unfaithfulness, gambling, overeating, or the abuse of alcohol, which in turn can cause marital or employment problems and can result in financial distress.

    - 1 John 2:15–16 says:

        > Do not love the world or the things in the world. If anyone loves the world, the love of the Father is not in him. For all that is in the world—the lust of the flesh, the lust of the eyes, and the pride of life—is not of the Father but is of the world. And the world is

passing away, and the lust of it; but he who does the will of God abides forever.

NKJV

- Galatians 5:16–21 says:

I say then: Walk in the Spirit, and you shall not fulfill the lust of the flesh. For the flesh lusts against the Spirit and the Spirit against the flesh; and these are contrary to one another, so that you do not do the things that you wish. But if you are led by the Spirit, you are not under the law. Now the works of the flesh are evident, which are: adultery, fornication, uncleanness, lewdness, idolatry, sorcery, hatred, contentions, jealousies, outbursts of wrath, selfish ambitions, dissensions, heresies, envy, murders, drunkenness, revelries, and the like; of which I tell you beforehand, just as I also told you in time past, that those who practice such things will not inherit the kingdom of God.

NKJV

- Ephesians 4:19 says, "Who, being past feeling, have given themselves over to lewdness, to work all uncleanness with greediness" (NKJV).

2. Pride and arrogance; to be preoccupied with one's own wisdom, accomplishments, power, abilities, reputation, or possessions: Pride makes us reluctant to admit our wrongs and reluctant to seek counsel. We will have a tendency to blame others for the problems that arise.

- Proverb 8:13 says, "The fear of the Lord is to hate evil; Pride and arrogance and the evil way and the perverse mouth I hate" (NKJV).
- 2 Corinthians 5:12 says, "For we do not commend ourselves again to you, but give you opportunity to glory on our behalf, that you may have an answer for those who boast in appearance and not in heart" (NKJV).
- James 3:14 says, "But if you have bitter envy and self-seeking in your hearts, do not boast and lie against the truth" (NKJV).

3. Love of money (other material possessions): It also appears as envy or an excessive desire for financial security. It can also make it difficult to forgive debts or show mercy.

- 1 Timothy 6:10 says, "For the love of money is a root of all kinds of evil, for which some have strayed from the faith in their greediness, and pierced themselves through with many sorrows" (NKJV).
- Ephesians 5:5 says, "For this you know, that no fornicator, unclean person, nor covetous man, who is an idolater, has any inheritance in the kingdom of Christ and God" (NKJV).

4. Fear of man (fear of what others can do to us); excessive concern about what others think about us.

- Luke 12:4–5 says, "And I say to you, My friends, do not be afraid of those who kill the body, and after that have no more that they can do. But I will show you whom you should fear: Fear him who, after he has killed, has power to cast into hell; yes, I say to you, fear him" (NKJV).

5. Good things that we want too much: The most difficult idols to deal with are good desires that we elevate to demands. These most subtle idols include love, happiness, good health, accomplishments, success, prosperity, recreation, goodwill, influence, status, a good image, or even spiritual power.

    - Luke 12:27–34 says:

      Consider the lilies, how they grow: they neither toil nor spin; and yet I say to you, even Solomon in all his glory was not arrayed like one of these. If then God so clothes the grass, which today is in the field and tomorrow is thrown into the oven, how much more will he clothe you, O you of little faith? And do not seek what you should eat or what you should drink, nor have an anxious mind. For all these things the nations of the world seek after, and your Father knows that you need these things. But seek the kingdom of God, and all these things shall be added to you. Do not fear, little flock, for it is your Father's good pleasure to give you the kingdom. Sell what you have and give alms; provide yourselves money bags which do not grow old, a treasure in the

> heavens that does not fail, where no thief approaches nor moth destroys. For where your treasure is, there your heart will be also.
>
> NKJV

Beware of these idols in your life. They are Satan's tools to promote failure in you! The enemy's attempt to promote division, contention, and discord in the body of Christ is always prevalent in the form of idol worship!

Remedy for destroying these hidden idols:

- Go back to chapter one and reread it. Review it.
- Identify with whose you are.
- Come to terms with who dwells in you.
- Repent.
- Ask the Lord to once again take up his throne in your heart.
- Get it in your spirit.

He has given us authority to render these idols inoperative in the life of the believer—in your life!

Luke 10:19 says, "Behold, I give you the authority to trample on serpents and scorpions, and over all the power of the enemy, and nothing shall by any means hurt you" (NKJV).

Yes, even though hidden idols in our lives open the door to the enemy for him to cause havoc through conflicts with others, we can be confident that we have the power to close that door by declaring God's Word and applying it to our lives. Conflict can be defeated just like these idols can be abolished by going back to what the Word of God says.

Make this declaration:

> I, ______________________, declare and decree that improper desires for physical pleasure, lust of flesh, pride and arrogance, the love of money, and the fear of man have no place in my heart, mind, and spirit. I declare that I am set free from their bondage in my life because you, Father, have given me authority over all the power of the enemy (Luke 10:19). Therefore, by the power of Christ that is vested in and through me, I render these idols ineffective and void in my life.

Today, I order these deceptive forces of the enemy inoperative in my life. I bind them according to Matthew 18:18, which says that whatever I bind and loose on earth will be bound and loosed in heaven. Therefore, I command these demonic forces to loose me and to return to the abyss and remain there! I release over my life what your Word says about me. I am more than a conqueror through Christ who strengthens me (Romans 8:37). I am the head and not the tail, the lender and not the borrower (Deuteronomy 28:13). My name has been written in the Lamb's Book of Life (Revelations 21:27). No weapon formed against me can prosper (Isaiah 54:17).

I have been adopted by the most High God (Ephesians 1:5) processor and Creator of the universe (Isaiah 40:28b). My name has been engraved in the very palms of your hands (Isaiah 49:16). You will never leave me or forsake me (Deuteronomy 31:8). I have been forgiven (1 John 1:9). You have blotted out my sin (Isaiah 44:22). I walk in the clarity of mind because I bring every thought captive to the obedience of who Christ is (2 Corinthians 5:10).

You have anointed me to preach the Gospel; to lay hands on the sick and they recover; the lame walk; the deaf hear; the blind see and the dead arise (Isaiah 61:1). You have anointed my eyes that I might walk by faith and not by sight (2 Corinthians 5:7). You have anointed my ears that I might have ears to hear what the Spirit of the Lord is saying to me (Revelation 3:22). You have anointed my mouth that I might speak words that edify, equip, and empower those around me, myself, and each other by being the doorkeeper to the entrance of my lips (Psalm 141:3). I walk in divine peace, the peace that passes all understanding (Philippians 4:7). Therefore, I walk free from the bondage of sin because he who the Son sets free is free indeed (John 8:36), in the name of Jesus Christ, the Son of the living God!

> Today, decide to render defeat, distractions, and demise, which fester in the confines of conflict, inoperative in your life and in the lives of your family and loved ones! Pray and declare triumph by rehearsing your victory today! Catch the vision of victory! Imagine yourself with victory in hand! Powerful! Conflict's adversary is called peace!

What Is Peace Management?

The previous chapter introduced the term *hidden idols*, what they are, and what forms they can take in our lives. We learned that they often are to blame for the sins we surrender to. Plus, they hinder and prevent our attempts for reconciliation and are responsible for triggering the conflicts we find ourselves in at times. We discovered what the Word of God had to say about them and their demise. We learned about conflict management and how to deal with conflict from both the secular view and biblical view. This chapter continues with the subject of conflict management by exploring and bringing to light the power we have in dealing with conflict from the standpoint of peace (to aid with healing and restoration).

The systematic theology for conflict management found in the Word of God I refer to is called peace management. When you apply it to your everyday life, it defeats the devil's schemes of dissension and strife every time!

The word *peace* means calm, quiet, stillness, tranquility, silence, serenity, and harmony. Peace management!

> **When you apply it to your everyday life, it defeats the devil's schemes of dissension and strife every time!**

Peace Management Approach

The peace management approach to resolving conflict is summarized in four basic godly principles shared in the book called *The Peace Maker*, by Ken Sande.

1. Glorifying God

   Biblical peacemaking is motivated and directed by a desire to please and honor God. His interests, reputations, and commands should take precedence over all other considerations. This focus not only shows our love and respect for God but also protects us from the impulsive, self-centered decisions that make conflicts even worse.

   First Corinthians 10:31 says, "Therefore, whether you eat or drink, or whatever you do, do all to the glory of God" (NKJV).

2. Getting the Log Out of Your Eye

   Peacemaking requires facing up to our own attitudes, faults, and responsibilities before pointing out what others have done wrong.

   Matthew 7:5 says, "Hypocrite! First remove the plank from your own eye, and then you will see clearly to remove the speck out of your brother's eye" (NKJV).

3. Going and Showing Your Brother His Fault

   At times, peacemaking also requires constructive confrontation. When others fail to accept responsibility for their actions, we may need to confront them in a gracious yet firm manner. If they refuse to respond appropriately, we may need to involve respected friends, church leaders, and other neutral individuals who can help restore peace.

   Matthew 18:15 says, "Moreover if your brother sins against you, go and tell him his fault between you and him alone. If he hears you, you have gained your brother" (NKJV).

4. Go and Be Reconciled

   Finally, peacemaking involves a commitment to restoring damaged relationships and developing agreements that are just and satisfactory to everyone involved. Forgiveness and cooperative negotiation clear away the debris left by conflict and make possible reconciliation and genuine peace.

   Matthew 5:24 says, "Leave your gift there before the altar, and go your way. First be reconciled to your brother, and then come and offer your gift"[29] (NKJV).

These principles are valuable and effective when applied and exercised in your Christian walk. They help to promote restoring resolutions to the conflicts, which can rob you of fulfilling your destiny. They also promote the promised guarantee of acquittal. Plus, they strengthen you for enduring in your transition from war to victory successfully.

Mr. Sande offers some powerful strategies for promoting peace when confronted with conflict founded in God's holy Word.

1. Speak Only to Build Up Others–Therefore, if you want to be an effective peacemaker, make a conscious effort to avoid reckless words, falsehood (e.g., hearsay, speculation, exaggeration, partial truths), gossip, slander, and other forms of worthless talk. A good way to avoid these types of speech is simply to talk less about others. As Proverbs 10:19 teaches, "When words are many, sin is not absent, but he who holds his tongue is wise" (NIV).

2. Be Quick to Listen–This element of effective communication is the ability to listen carefully to what others are saying. Probably because this is not a skill that comes naturally to most of us, James gave this warning to the early church: "My dear brothers, take note of this: Everyone should be quick to listen, slow to speak and slow to become angry" (James 1:19, NIV).

3. Heal With Wise Communication–The ability to confront others in a clear, constructive, and persuasive manner. Proverbs 12:18 is particularly relevant to this task: "Reckless words pierce like a sword, but the tongue of the wise brings healing" (NIV).[30]

Recently, I had an opportunity to put into practice some of the techniques shared in this chapter for confronting conflict when I was called upon to minister in the scenario below. These principles proved to be an asset in promoting a solution for healing and restoration to take place.

As an author and speaker for the cause of Christ, I am often challenged in my relationships to minister to those who find themselves in disputes and disagreements. I received such a call from someone who seemed very upset over an exchange of words she had experienced with another. She wanted advice on how to remedy the situation.

I paused a moment after listening to her and asked, "Can God see his reflection in you?"

To which she replied, "I'm not sure."

Then I responded with the principles "Speak the Truth in Love" (as outlined above). Soon after applying these trustworthy principles founded in God's Word to her situation, the misunderstanding was resolved with no injury to either party. Their relationship began to blossom. They were on speaking terms and able to establish a mutual sense of respect and trust in their relationship with each other.

Keep in mind that a peacemaker bears the highest penalty and greatest cost. It is important to also note that when the strategists weigh the difference between war and peace, the ones who are secure in their beliefs and are confident of the win often choose peace as their ally regardless of the cost and or penalty. Why? Because peace proves an earned champion and its residue leaves one wiser, with a greater sensitivity for the needs of others whose sacrifices are honored through peace, liberty, and love found in unity.

> Jesus depends on unity! Unity is more than a key to internal peace. It is also an essential element of your Christian witness. When peace and unity characterize your relationships with other people, you show that God is present in your life. The converse is also true; when your life is filled with unresolved conflict, you will have little success in sharing the Good News about Jesus Christ.[31]

This systematic godly perspective allows us the escape route for running the race and living life in a masterful way while taking notice of the finish line, which seems to shout to the one who crosses it, "You've triumphed!" This kind of victory is not temporary, but everlasting because its foundation is Christ. Its rewards of restoration and reconciliation are eternally given by him found in our obedience and commitment to practice his statutes and endure.

For peace proves an earned champion, and its residue leaves one wiser, with a greater sensitivity for the needs of others.

Notably, the contents of the Bible continue to inflict each generation, as with the past one, with his central message to cause change and restoration in those exposed to them (those who choose to accept them at face value). It is important that we refrain from finding new religious, ritualistic angles to presenting his truths. It will avoid the consequences of doing so, which tear at the fabric of God's standards of faith, validity, and security found in his uncensored, detailed, Holy Spirit inspired gospel.

- We can rely on the truths of scripture to lead us and guide us in how we choose to live our lives and forgo living of our lives through the opinions of another.
- We can guard our God-given revelations of his truth and limit exposing our intellect to the enticements of the many misconceptions of his Word.
- We can maintain our focus on the simplicity of the central theme of Scripture: "The Son of God, from a virgin birth, the Redeemer" of mankind by the shedding of his blood, all accomplished for the purpose of reconciling mankind to God.

> **It is the foundation that transforms opinions into divine revelation.**

Admirably, the Word of God is alive and never changes because he never changes. The old cliché comes to mind: "History repeats itself." The Word of God will not pass away! Matthew 24:35 says, "Heaven and earth will pass away, but My words will by no means pass away" (NKJV).

It is the foundation of his Word that transforms opinions into divine revelation. These revelations withstand the unforgiving erosion of the decades we have spent in the agonizing pursuit of the analytical matters of this world. First Corinthians 3:18–21 says:

> Let no one deceive himself. If anyone among you seems to be wise in this age, let him become a fool that he may become wise. For the wisdom of this world is foolishness with God. For it is written,

> "He catches the wise in their own craftiness" and again, the Lord knows the thoughts of the wise, that they are futile.
>
> NKJV

It is only when we seek him that we are truly blessed with his immeasurable wisdom to cause transformation from our broken lives to that of wholeness through him and promote a significant, everlasting difference in this world.

To seek him, one must be awake and alert to his demands, commands, and guidance for upholding his statutes. Our bridegroom calls upon us to take our rightful position as his bride. Therefore, we must comply in order to meet the terms our responsibility as his chosen bride.

Thus says the Lord:

> **Be careful that you do not get caught up in the contemporary Christian crusade. For they only want, want, want, but I am here to tell you that they shall have their reward. For I have called you to a higher place with me; one of greater responsibility; one of example; one of passion for me and all I represent; everything, not just what they believe I should be. Reach out and touch my people. Heed their cry. Understand my command and take heed. For my kingdom is at hand, and I have chosen you for today, for such a time, to defeat the devil and raise my banners of victory and righteousness. I am holy, so be holy. Accept nothing less than all that I have for you. For great shall be your reward.**
>
> **The word of the Lord,**
> **spoken to my heart**

Pastors Only

I know we have covered a great deal of ground. And yes, I discern at times it has been difficult to digest some of the material shared because it has dealt with issues that, quite frankly, are sensitive. Issues of this nature have often been better left alone in the past. But this is precisely what needs to happen if we are going to be prepared to meet our bridegroom one day. Hopefully, it has provoked you to consider an examination of your thoughts, ideals, and mindset. As you know, the Word of God is clear on the subject of self-examination and the benefits therein one stands to experience as a result.

Second Corinthians 13:5–6 says,

> Examine yourselves to see whether you are in the faith; test yourselves. Do you not realize that Christ Jesus is in you-unless, of course, you fail the test? And I trust that you will discover that we have not failed the test.
>
> NIV

I congratulate you for your persistence and desire to overcome and succeed in leadership and ministry. I am overjoyed that you have chosen to see this project through. Hopefully, you have gleaned from its pages some applicable wisdom for your ministry and some information to encourage you in the area of healing and restoration ministry.

Now, come face to face with a powerful word, he spoke to my heart. I am not sure why he chose me, but these words of truth validate and demonstrate God's desire for you and me to succeed in ministry! One morning during the month of August 2003, God woke me up at about four o'clock a.m. and whispered, *I have something for you; write this down.* Truly powerful and humbling! He had me title the information "Pastors Only," so I began to write.

1. *You were made white as snow at the time of salvation: you must maintain your garment free from spot and wrinkle!* Isaiah 1:18: "'Come now, and let us reason together, says the Lord, 'Though your sins are like scarlet, they shall be as white as snow'" (NKJV). Ephesians 5:27: "That He might present her to himself a glorious church, not having spot or wrinkle or any such thing, but that she should be holy and without blemish" (NKJV).

2. *Stop diluting the anointing in fulfilling the call to the ministry. The devil's purpose is to cause you to dilute its power with distractions within the ministry. Beware!* The anointing on you can be divided and dispersed among things other than what it is purposed for.

An example of a person who did just that was Aaron, Moses's brother. He was anointed to speak, and the people listened. Aaron, evidently a man of influence already among the Israelites, introduced Moses to their assembled elders and as his mouthpiece declared to them the divine commission of Moses with such persuasive power under the Spirit that the people "believed, bowed their heads, and worshiped" Exodus 4:29–31. (From Fausset's Bible Dictionary, Electronic Database Copyright 1998 by Biblesoft.)

On the other hand, Aaron's speaking anointing was misused by him and sadly caused the people of Israel to sin greatly in the sight of God! Exodus 32:1–6 says:

> And Aaron said to them, "Break off the golden earrings which are in the ears of your wives, your sons, and your daughters, and bring them to me." So all the people broke off the golden earrings which were in their ears, and brought them to Aaron. And he received the gold from their hand, and he fashioned it with an engraving tool, and made a molded calf.
>
> NKJV

3. *The ministry will always belong to me. The call is yours.*
4. *Stop ministering when I am ministering to you by my Holy Spirit anointing! When the anointing falls in the house, partake of it!* It guarantees the sanctification of the house. For all that is not of me to be consumed (Isaiah 45:8). The anointing and My presence keeps the house purified. *It is not by your works of righteousness that the sanctu-*

ary maintains its pure state or by your convictions (Malachi 3:3 and 1 Corinthians 3:12–15).

5. *Stop controlling your congregation!* (1 Peter 5:1–4)
6. *Do not prostitute my Word by diluting it!*
7. *Do not compromise my Word by allowing your tithers to influence your messages!* First Timothy 5:21 says, "I charge you, in the sight of God and Christ Jesus and the elect angels, to keep these instructions without partiality, and to do nothing out of favoritism" (NIV).
8. *Stop fighting over congregation members and between churches!* (Mark 16:15)
9. *Teach on giving!*
10. *Tithe goes to the overseer of your soul* (Numbers 18:23–24)
    A. Offering is for establishing a good work (Deuteronomy 8:18)
    B. Giving to the poor (Luke 6:32–36)
11. *Do not confuse gratitude with glory!* Reward those you are in charge of.
    - Gratitude–1 Timothy 5:17
    - Glory belongs to me
12. *Share your pulpit! You do not know it all. It is crucial for Me to stir up the gifts in you and in the potential evangelists, apostles, prophets, teachers, and pastors in your congregations. They must be anointed* (quickened) *by those I send to you, who are gifted in the other offices of ministry. I want you*

well rounded, and I want your congregations well equipped. You must expose yourself and your congregation to the five offices of the gospel.

13. *Ask yourself, "Why is my church not growing?"* Is it because you are comfortable with the size and the figures of your church? *Examine yourself* (2 Corinthians 13:5). Your number-one priority should be souls!
14. *Guard yourselves against pride and giving no love.*
15. *Do not pass onto your congregation your personal convictions. I am trying to grow you in a specific area to cause you to become well rounded.*
16. *Stop trying to become righteous! You already are!* Nothing you do on the outside of your body will make you more righteous. You have my righteousness upon you!
17. *Stop separating the men and women in the church! Teach both, for they are one. Do not forget to teach the children for they are the generation I will use to usher in the return of My Son.*
18. *Do not allow the congregation to make a god out of you!*

In bewilderment, I contemplated his list. I was not a pastor, and I could not understand why he shared such specifics about ministering as one. Several days later, in prayer, I received the second part of my assignment: *Visit different churches, one per week for three months and take notes, such as, Do they allow the Holy Spirit to abide in their church? Do they worship and praise freely? Do they take tithes and offer-*

ings? What are they teaching? Then I am going to send you to places of worship to share your findings.

To my dismay, I found areas of opportunities in some of the churches I visited and observed. These findings paved the way for me to document them and expose the spot of pride and the wrinkle called lack of love to those who will have ears to hear.

This project serves as a warning sign, if you will, to watch out for! It is filled with powerful strategies and remedies needed for eliminating the spot and wrinkle on her bridal dress in order to prepare her effectively for the bridegroom's arrival.

As you already have come to know, the devil is unrelenting in causing the church to stumble in the darkness of his ploys, lies, and manipulating schemes. His mission is to cripple our every effort to maintain our integrity as Jesus's unblemished bride to be!

> Recently, during a visit of a local church, I found myself listening to a sermon called "The Jezebel Spirit." After much debate from the pulpit on the subject, I realized that during these times of such darkness, the term *Jezebel spirit* has been identified as the culprit when confronted by situations that seem to encompass discourse and havoc. For example, division in the church and/or the decline of reached souls in a church is now being attributed to the Jezebel spirit. Who is this Jezebel spirit? And where does it come from? What about you? Have you heard this term before?

Now, direct your attention with me at exposing the Jezebel spirit by identifying its destructive ploys and effects within the four walls of the church. First, this new phenomenon known as the Jezebel spirit plaguing our churches today has been diligently at work for a long time, way back from provoking the fall of man in the garden of Eden, to provoking the chaos, division, and dissension we are experiencing in the body of Christ today.

Jezebel has been working hard, devising new techniques for inflicting doubt and conflict. Her cunning manipulation of Christian applications is aimed at binding us to what we think is our God-given purpose for decades! She (the Jezebel spirit) is alive and well today!

The Old Testament describes the Jezebel spirit as visible in Jezebel, the manipulative wife of King Ahab. The name *Jezebel* is defined as unexalted, unhusbanded.[32]

Through her craftiness and cunningness, Queen Jezebel singlehandedly killed hundreds of God's prophets and managed to induce three-quarters of the nation of Israel to turn from worshiping God to the worship of the god of Baal.

First Kings 19:14, 18 says:

> And he [the prophet Elijah] said, "I have been very zealous for the Lord God of hosts; because the children of Israel have forsaken Your covenant, torn down Your altars, and killed your prophets with the sword. I alone am left; and they seek to take my life. Yet [God says], I have reserved seven thousand in Israel, all whose knees have not bowed to Baal, and every mouth that has not kissed him."
>
> AMP

This spirit manifested itself greatly in Queen Jezebel. The traits and characteristics she possessed gave way for this spirit to operate effectively through her. The name *Jezebel* translated from the Greek means "without cohabitation."[33]

To be without cohabitation, one must desire to be alone or only be in the company of those one can control. Queen Jezebel operated in control, deceit, and corruptive influence. She was seductive and dealt deadly ploys to accomplish her plan. She was daughter of King Ethbaal of Sidon.

Sidon was a city of great commerce on the coast of the Mediterranean Sea. The city of Sidon can be better understood in its compatibility to Sodom and Gomorrah. It was full of vices and malice. King Ahab of Israel married Jezebel and brought her to the land of Israel as his queen. She then decided to take residence in the city of Jezreel, a city that served God.

Soon thereafter, her deceitful plan to convert the city of Jezreel into her native hometown of Sidon began to unfold. Queen Jezebel pursued her new venture with the worship of the golden calf. She convinced the king of his need to join her in her desire to worship Jehovah God with it. "Actually, the calf was a central idol in the worship of Baal, a sun god who was important to ancient Phoenicians. Because Baal was believed to have power over crops, flocks, and the fertility of farm families, the gold calf was often linked with him."[34] The worship of Baal took the nation of Israel by storm, and soon many temples were erected for those loyal to pagan worship. "The worship of Baal took the form of human sacrifice, self-torture, sexual immorality, fertility rituals, and the kissing of its image. Queen Jezebel caused Israel to sin greatly in the sight of God. In her effort to erase the mark of Jehovah throughout Israel, Jezebel became the first female religious persecutor in Bible history."[35]

> Although, this spirit chose the queen, a woman, to inject its vicious idolatry appetite into the veins of Israel, it is important to note that it is a spirit with no gender. Even though we have come to grips with its identity as that of a female gender in the body of Christ, we must not exclude the possibility of the male gender being used in like manner to destroy, divide, and control the present church. "Jezebel (spirit) is more attracted to the uniqueness of the female psyche in its sophisticated ability to manipulate without physical force."[36] Whether female or male, this spirit's only agenda is to oppose the works of God and his existence as the great I AM.
>
> The Jezebel spirit manifested in adversaries throughout history took the form of males such as King Antiochus IV. He was responsible for the killing of Jewish men and enslaving their women and children. He also instituted capital punishment for those who practiced the Mosaic Law. This king desired to control those around him with an iron fist. He forced those under his rule to practice paganism.

It became a capital offense to practice circumcision, observe the Sabbath, celebrate Jewish festivals, or possess scrolls of Old Testament books. Many holy scrolls were destroyed. Pagan sacrifices became compulsory, as did processional marching in honor of Dionysus (or Bacchus), the Greek god of wine. An altar to the Syrian high god, identified as Zeus, was erected in the Jewish temple.[37]

> Still, there were others who were possessed in the same likeness of Jezebel. There were emperors and kings of the first century who claimed deity while still alive. Their names were Caligula and Domitian. Emperor Caligula ordered a statue of himself to be placed in the Jewish temple to be worshipped after his death. Emperor Domitian expected and forced those under his rule to worship him. Many Christians and Jews alike who refused to participate in what others considered patriotic duty suffered great persecution.
>
> King Herod, the king of Judea, was no different; he also believed himself supreme and worthy of homage. He caused great affliction upon the Jews during the time of Jesus' birth. In the likeness of Jezebel, he managed to murder their male children under the age of two in the city of Bethlehem. It was an attempt to annihilate the newborn king of the Jews, the prophesied Messiah, from the city of Bethlehem.

The Jezebel spirit has and will continue to be a threat to those who choose to embrace God. We must come to terms with it, identify it, and purpose in our hearts to evade its fiery darts. It is a very powerful force the enemy has used to cause conflict within the fortresses of religion, from the ancient temples of the Jews to the modern churches of today.

Ask yourself: Is Jezebel operating in my church?

Is Jezebel Operating in Your Church?

How do we identify Jezebel in our churches? The evidence that Jezebel is at work in any church or any ministry is best described by its effects. When it has infiltrated and injected its vicious venom of strongholds, it is felt by the body of Christ.

> A person operating in a Jezebel spirit will seek to teach church doctrine in order to gain a controlling grip on the body. These doctrines will be incomplete, inaccurate, and full of holes. Scripture will usually be taken out of context and misapplied. Even if the person's teachings begin correctly, in time it will deteriorate because it has no deep root. Gradually, a transition will occur. Progressively, the Bible will be ignored, and mystical ways will take a more prominent role.[38]

Another strong sensation or indication that division, strife, and ultimate destruction of the ministry, if not recognized, is at the hand of Jezebel occurs when the deadly venom of these four strongholds manifest themselves in the leadership in the form of:

1. Pride
2. Self-righteousness
3. Lust for the things of this world and/or a craving for satisfying a sexual appetite
4. Unforgiveness

Word to the wise: We have the power to identify Jezebel and put a stop to her craftiness by implementing the peace management approach, principles, and strategies found in chapter five and by educating ourselves in the ability to recognize her targets of attack, preventing her from destroying the existing works of ministry in the body of Christ.

The book of Revelation speaks of the spirit of Jezebel. It is in the midst of the prophesied battle between good and evil called Armageddon. The apostle John is given a vision of future events that will affect the outcome of life as we know it. In the vision, Jesus is addressing one of the seven churches, appraising the roles each one has played as the bride, the body of Christ. He speaks to the one called Thyatira.

Revelation 2:19–20 says:

> I know your works, love, service, faith and your patience; and as for your works, the last are more than the first. Nevertheless, I have a few things against you, because you allow that woman Jezebel, who calls herself a prophetess, to teach and seduce My servants to commit sexual immorality and eat things sacrifice to idols.
>
> NKJV

The generational battle history between good and evil has given us a picture of how Satan uses her to destroy the body of Christ from within the walls of religion. However, we have the ability to assimilate from her past attempts her detailed attack pattern to combat her every move!

Take note: She has proven to be attracted to those in leadership positions. They are most vulnerable! "Prayer leaders, church secretaries, worship and song leaders, pastors and wives, are especially targeted by this spirit."[39] The Jezebel characteristics are rebellion, manipulation, control, and hate.

Her traits are seductiveness, un-cohabitation, and tolerance to compromise.

What Is Jezebel's Desire?

Be aware! Identify the chaff and destroy it before it impacts the wheat. If we are to be productive for the kingdom of God, we cannot allow the brilliance of our wedding garment to be tainted or blemished by Jezebel. Gaining insight about her will cause us to take hold of the strategic godly weapons of warfare that exist in his Word. Plus, it will activate the usage of them (the weapons of warfare) in our lives to prevent us from falling into Jezebel's claws of destruction.

God's Weapons of Choice in Promoting Jezebel's Demise

> What are God's weapons of choice in promoting Jezebel's demise?

"Jezebel's worst enemies are the prophets; her worst fear is that the people will embrace repentance. She hates repentance."[40]

God's weapons of choice are:

1. Repentance
2. Humility

3. Intercessory prayer
4. The word of your testimony
5. Praise and worship

There is great power available to us in his Word!

- Meekness
- Humility
- Our diligence to submit
- Being accountable to one another (incorporates the truth in the power of leadership roles).
- Intercessory prayer

These are powerful allies in dealing with Jezebel!

Intercessory teams and intercessory prayer are important aids in gaining insight into the schemes of the enemy before his grip is felt. These strategic maneuvers are important in defusing and exposing the wiles of the enemy targeted at the body of Christ. "Jezebel hates prayer. Intercessory prayer pries her fingers off the hearts and souls of men."[41]

The word of our testimony brings glory to God for who he is and what he has accomplished in and through our lives. Our confessions can cause a great deal of damage to the image of Jezebel because they focus all of the attention on God, not on her. It is imperative that we use these powerful weapons of warfare that our Father has outlined in the Word to put Jezebel out of commission in our churches!

Our heavenly Father has always chosen those who

could do battle with the spirit of Jezebel (as proven by history) to bring it to nothing in any given situation. In the body of Christ, there are selected ones with the call on their lives to destroy and expose this spirit within their church. God has strategically placed the Elijahs, Jehus, and eunuchs in place who will not submit to the seductiveness of Jezebel! Keep this in mind! Do not fear!

Elijah the prophet portrayed in the book of 2 Kings was instrumental in destroying the false prophets, as well as the satanic priests ordained by Queen Jezebel in Israel. In all, there were 850 men killed in one day by the order of Elijah (the prophet). Jehu, a ruler of the longest-lived dynasty in Israel came later to do battle against Jezebel herself. He was given the assignment by God to eliminate her (2 Kings 9:7).

Her servants were the eunuchs, who were not affected by her feminine seductiveness and therefore responded to Jehu's command for them to throw her to her death off the balcony of her palace.

Are you one of these: a Jehus, eunuch or an Elijah?

Let us examine ourselves today! We are called by God to stand as one of these in our churches, to arm ourselves with the precious weaponry he provides:

1. Love
2. Prayer, intercessory prayer
3. Praise and worship, declaring victory
4. Walking in forgiveness

5. A penitent heart
6. An attitude of repentance
7. Covered in his righteousness

Although the threat of the Jezebel spirit is real, we can follow the example of the eunuchs who betrayed Jezebel. They did so because they had been castrated and set apart for servitude. "To topple Satan's empire, we are to be transformed into Christ's likeness."[42] We are to circumcise our hearts and consecrate ourselves by setting ourselves apart for our bridegroom and master, the Savior of our souls, to defeat the enticements of Jezebel.

We Can Learn to Be Steadfast in Our Commitment!

We can learn to be steadfast! Then the enemy will have to flee. Make a decision today to give her no chance of occupying your position in the church. Remember, Jezebel cannot invade your territory if you are lined up with his statutes, wearing his armor of righteousness with his sword (the Word) firmly nestled in the palm of your hand.

Yes, even though it is quite clear that the Jezebel spirit has made a mark in history in our present churches and very possibly will do the same in the future, it still remains our responsibility to educate ourselves in the many crafty methods and devices at work within this spirit. Why? So we can be on the lookout for those who choose to work and walk within its boundaries.

It is vital to the strength and growth of God's kingdom that we take our rightful place in the body of Christ and identify with whose we are! It is when we understand who we are in Christ Jesus and come to terms with the power of his righteousness that we can overcome the enemy! Luke 10:19 says he has given us authority over all the power of the enemy.

Therefore, we can fight the many enticements of pursuing the estranged, mangled, and repulsive convictions of a contemporary world religion with its procedures and purpose to seek out instead the eternal benefits of restoration and healing found in the uncompromised statutes set before us in his Word.

Thus says the Lord:

> **In self-righteousness, through justification in your path, your light has become dim. No! No! No! Let my righteousness cover you to lead you to the center of my will for your lives. Then your light will shine brightly. Then the blind without salvation will see the light in you and will find their path to salvation.**
>
> **—Word from the Lord spoken to my heart**

Are you ready to stand fast, rooted in his perfect will for your life, by committing today to wait on him, no matter what? Remind yourself now that you can accomplish that which is required of you because he is with you, working through you. Therefore, stand and be counted at attention and witness the salvation of the Lord! I know it is a great deal to absorb from knowing who you are (his chosen bride) to defining sin, Christian conditional behavior, conflict management, peace management, and last but not least, identifying with the Jezebel spirit! But in doing so, you are being exposed to the spots and wrinkles that can often lay dormant in the confines of our dress due to the darkness of the times. Therefore, it is important that we become aware of their existence in order to promote a bride that is vigilant in her effort to please her bridegroom.

Ministers Share Their Strategies

After completing this project, I was led to approach five successful ministries with three questions in hopes they would answer them to encourage and educate us in ministry. I am thrilled to have received their input.

This group of ministers shares its strategies. Their diversity uniquely empowers them to share their views on healing and restoration in the body of Christ today. This information is vital to the bride of Christ because it provides additional answers to the much-needed healing and restoration we must embrace in order to fulfill our purpose as his bride. It is in a large way the conclusion to this project, the visible efforts made in her desire to present herself as a bride without spot or wrinkle, based on the foundational truths of the Bible. These five ministries offer valuable information for heading successful restoration and healing ministries, which can make a great difference in the way we minister to each other and those who choose the confines of our churches in search of answers.

T.D. Jakes, named by *Time* magazine America's best preacher, Pastor Sunday of the largest church in Europe, Dr. Dick Rueben with Evangelistic Association, and Pastor Shaffer, a pastors' pastor, all share their thoughts in letter form. Plus, Rabbi Brawer (a Jewish believer) answers the three questions by agreeing to an interview. Here is what they had to say. First, the letters and their contents, and then I conclude with the interview with Rabbi Brawer.

Bishop T.D. Jakes

"He is a virtuoso, a prodigy. The only thing more exhilarating than the style of T.D. Jakes's sermons is their rigor and compassion" (*Time* magazine, September 2001).

Biography

Pastor, community advocate, humanitarian, author, songwriter, playwright, conference speaker, and broadcaster, Bishop Thomas D. Jakes Sr. was born on June 9, 1957, in South Charleston, West Virginia. His parents, businessman and entrepreneur Ernest Sr. and educator Judith were charitable benefactors in their community and to whom their son credits for his own integrity, discipline, and self-reliance. From a very young age, he was devoted to the gospel, and in 1979, Bishop Jakes began fulfilling his call to the ministry by founding and serving as pastor of Greater Emmanuel Temple of Faith, a small storefront church in Montgomery, West Virginia, which originated with only ten members.

Now, twenty years later as a pastor and some twenty-five years later serving in the ministry, he pastors what *Christianity Today* calls "one of America's fastest growing mega-churches." Named The Potter's House, this multi-racial, non-denominational church with fifty-nine active internal and outreach ministries has dominated church growth records since 1996. In only five years since relocating the church from West Virginia to Dallas, Texas, The Potter's House grew from fifty families to more than twenty-eight thousand members to date.

In January 1999, the New York Times named Bishop T.D. Jakes as "one of the top five evangelists most frequently cited by scholars, theologians, and evangelical leaders to step up the international pulpit behind the Reverend Billy Graham," while *Time* magazine featured Bishop Jakes on a September 2001 cover and named him "America's best preacher."

Often referred to as a "shepherd to the shattered," Bishop Jakes has made great strides in Dallas to help turn around the lives of the homeless, drug addicts, prostitutes, single mothers, and others in life-threatening circumstances. In addition, The Potter's House has created programs such as The Guardians, an outreach to the homeless; Rahab International, an outreach to prostitutes and women in abusive domestic situations; a GED literacy program; the Transformation Treatment Program for drug and alcohol abusers; an AIDS outreach; and a prison outreach. A devoted advocate of religious outreach to prison inmates, Bishop Jakes has been to several prisons to minister in person, most recently at a three-day summer crusade at San Quentin. He also created The Potter's House Prison Satellite Network, which provides gospel programming to more than 375 prisons in forty states, earns a viewership more than 350,000 inmates.

To reach the greater religious community, Bishop T.D. Jakes preaches the gospel on his national weekly television broadcast, "The Potter's House" on the Trinity Broadcasting Network (TBN), Black Entertainment Television (BET), and the Daystar Network. He broadcasts to international audiences weekly via the Inspiration Network, Christian Channel Europe, and the God Channel. His other weekly program is "The Potter's Touch," a daily thirty-minute talk show that focuses on many of the pressing topics and situations that affect the church and the body of Christ. It is seen on both the Trinity Broadcasting Network and Black Entertainment Television.

Bishop Jakes is the CEO of The Potter's House Ministries, a nonprofit organization that produces three major national conferences: The Pastor's and Leadership Conference, ManPower, and "Woman, Thou Art Loosed!" WTAL, a powerful and popular symposium for women that addresses the pain of women of all races and ages, has set national indoor attendance records with 84,500 attendees and an additional 20,000 in overflow at the Georgia Dome in 1999.

Dear Rev. Salmonson,

Please see below the answers you requested from Bishop Jakes. Once again, we appreciate your interest in his ministry.

1. What is your perspective of the condition of the body of Christ today in terms of being a healing and restoring body?

I believe that in the midst of a stormy society, the body of Christ is strengthening. The Word of God is being preached all over the world. People are hearing the Gospel as never before. I believe that Christians are seeking God as never before. Psalm 107:19–20 states that if we cry unto the Lord, he will hear us and send his Word and heal us and deliver us from our destructions. I believe that the Lord is hearing us and is moving.

The body of Christ is beginning to look beyond barriers of race, ethnicity, and socioeconomic status to reach across to bring help to the hurting. Certainly the church has a long way to go to actually fulfilling Christ's call to "love our neighbor as ourselves," (Matthew 22:39), but as we are more and more faithful, God is enabling us to be a healing and restorative force in the church and in the world.

2. What key principles have you put in place in your church for being a successful healing and restoring church?

We believe that God's ultimate purpose for us is winning souls to him. Through that quest, we have implemented more than fifty ministries to assist us in healing and restoring people, as well as the community outside of our church. Our Transformation Center is a licensed drug and alcohol program designed to restore adults and families affected by chemical dependency.

The goal of the prison ministry here at The Potter's House is to aid in the restoration of the lives of offenders through the infusion of intellectual, emotional, and spiritual influence. We also aim to help them avoid addictive and destructive relationships and behaviors, stay out of prison, and become positive contributors to society.

We also have professional Christian counselors available through our counseling department. Its function is to integrate biblical truths with clinical procedures to assist each individual seeking spiritual and emotional wholeness. Our singles ministry, title P.H.A.S.E., which stands for patient, holy, anointed, single, and entirely, motivates and stimulates today's single body of believers to further know the Lord Jesus Christ. These programs are a representation of the many other services we provide to the homeless, as well as other ministries.

It is important we provide a place where people can be honest about where they are in their spiritual growth. It is also important when working with these cases that their privacy and progress be protected. Often those who have received help are able to help others through the process once they have their healing.

3. What advice could you offer to a new pastor beginning a new work in the area of healing and restoration?

I would advise a pastor to commit to brutal honesty with himself in assessing the health of his flock. Don't be afraid to say, "We've got a long way to go to be a healing and restorative body." Commit to God's vision to get you from where you are to where he wants you to go. Trust him to make yours a mighty part of his kingdom. And pray! Pray! Pray! Pray!

Warmest Regards,

—Carolyn Miller
Director of Public Relations
Office of Public Relations
The Potter's House of Dallas, Inc.

Biography
Pastor Sunday

Pastor Sunday, as he is called by the members of the church, has an international ministry that reaches to over thirty

countries, including the USA, Canada, England, Germany, Russia, Singapore, Kazakhstan, Nigeria, Holland, Indonesia, Spain, South Africa, Latvia, Israel, Sweden, Estonia, Norway, South Korea, Kyrgyzstan, Denmark, and many others. He speaks in many city, state, region, and countrywide conferences, sharing the word of encouragement and instruction that the Lord has given him.

Pastor Sunday is used mightily in prophetic and evangelistic gifts around the world. God's gift of healing flows through Pastor Sunday and countless people have been healed, restored, and set free by his ministry.

Pastor Sunday is not only an international speaker and pastor of the largest church (20,000 members) in Europe, but he is also a loving husband to Bose Adelaja and the responsible and happy father of three children, a son, Perez, and two daughters, Zoe and Pearl. Pastor Bose Adelaja is a fitting helpmate for Pastor Sunday, and their gifts and callings complement each other perfectly. Whenever possible, Pastor Sunday travels with his wife and children.

Pastor Sunday's letter had this to say:

> Dear Reverend Salmonson,
>
> Here are the answers to the questions you asked for:
>
> 1. What is your perspective of the condition of the body of Christ today in terms of being a healing and restoring body?
>
> My perspective about the body of Christ in terms of being a healing and restoring body is not as bad as it used to be when there were few charismatic churches who practiced healing and restoration. Today is much better because there are a lot of

churches that have now experienced the charismatic renewal and thanks to this renewal, mainline churches have also tasted of the healing power of the Lord. However, there is still a lot to be done and a long distance to go. I think too many believers are not aware of the authority they have in the Lord so that they themselves can deal with the challenges in the area of healing, deliverance, and restoration. I think the ultimate goal of God is for every believer to find for himself what the Lord has for him and walk in that truth by faith and through the knowledge of the Holy Spirit; we will have fewer problems and challenges in dealing with the sick and weary in the church.

John 8:32 says, "And ye shall know the truth, and the truth shall make you free," and 1 Peter 2:24 says, "Who his own self bare our sins in his own body on the tree that we, being dead to sins, should live unto righteousness: by whose stripes ye were healed." I think the church needs to do a better job in teaching and training believers to walk as overcomers in truth and redemption.

2. What principles have you put in place in your church for being a successful healing and restoring church?

The principles God has taught us in being a healing and successful church are diverse. The most important is to lay sound and penetrating teaching on the truth of the Word of God. We teach that, as believers, we have authority in the Word of the Lord.

This teaching takes place on different levels, starting with the senior pastor on down to the home groups and different outreaches of our church. We have launched several departments to minister to the needy in the area of healing and restoration. For example, Monday to Saturday, between twelve noon and six p.m., we hold healing classes where people come to be prayed for and get teaching. Another ministry similar to that is prayer for the salvation of relatives and family members. We also have a ministry dealing with drug and alcohol addicts. All these ministries function every day and are ready to answer people's questions and meet their needs. Apart from this, we have a special healing service every Sunday where, from the main platform, one of our pastors ministers to all who are in need of healing and restoration. We encourage our people to be a stream of healing to their neighbors.

3. What advice could you offer to a new pastor beginning a new work in the area of healing and restoration?

The advice I would like to offer to a new pastor beginning a new work in the area of healing and restoration would, first of all, be to study the subject very well, to get well prepared for the task ahead. Knowledge of the Word of God will bring the faith that he needs to minister to the people. Secondly, before he can minister to others, he must be stronger than the enemy in the spirit realm, stronger than Satan who brought sickness and destruction to this world. He must be able to deal with the enemy properly and really be spiritually grounded in the Lord. In Luke 11:14–22, the Bible tells us the story of a man who tried to bind the strongman. If you plan to bind the strongman, you must be stronger. For you to be stronger than the enemy, you must exercise in regular prayer and fasting and walk with the Lord in intimacy with the Holy Spirit. With that, you should be able to cope with many challenges in the area of healing.

The next thing I feel a new pastor needs is great compassion. Without compassion for people, our prayers are helpless and weak. Compassion is necessary in the area of healing. I recommend taking some ideas from the previous question (above) to help you to practically begin in ministry when the time comes.

Regards,

—Pastor Sunday

Biography
Dr. Dick Reuben, Evangelistic Association International

Being Jewish is not an easy task in an anti-Semitic world, especially if you are a born-again Christian or Messianic Jew. The *Ruach Elohim* (Spirit of the living God) overcame all the odds of a Jew ever becoming a believer when Brother Reuben became Dr. Dick Reuben, a believer in Yeshua, the promised Messiah of Israel, on the evening of March 1, 1971. He gave his heart to the Lord at a Rex Humbard crusade in Norfolk, Virginia. That night, an outlaw biker that society had written off as a habitual loser was radically saved and called by the grace and mercy of the Almighty God of Abraham, Isaac, and Jacob.

Dick Reuben entered full time ministry in 1985 and was a pastor of a small church in Indiana for several years before becoming a traveling evangelist. Having studied under a noted Messianic rabbi for six years, Brother Reuben attended the Institute of Ministry in Bradenton, Florida, and Christ for the Nations in Dallas, Texas. He joined the staff of Rock of Israel in January of 1990 as a field representative with the Assemblies of God home missions in Southern California. Brother Reuben received his DD degree from (and for a short time taught at) the Southern California Theological Seminary as a professor of Old Testament theology.

Today, Dr. Reuben travels around the world with his wife and faithful companion, Deanne, by his side with offices and representatives throughout the world.

Dr. Dick Rueben stated the following in his response:

> Dear Sis: Marilyn,
>
> Here are the answers to the questions...
>
> 1. What is your perspective of the condition of the body of Christ today in terms of being a healing and restoring body?
>
> The restoration of the healing balm of God's anointing can only come when the theological sword of

the Lord is wheeled upon the powers of darkness and not upon the backs of fellow believers.

The prayer for unity prayed by Jesus for his disciples was prayed as follows.

"Neither pray I for these alone, but for them also which shall believe on me through their word; That they all may be one; as thou, Father, art in me, and I in thee, that they also may be one in us: that the world may believe that thou hast sent me" (John 17:20–21).

Unity was likened unto the anointing oil flowing freely running down upon the High Priest Aaron's garments.

"Behold, how good and how pleasant it is for brethren to dwell together in unity! It is like the precious ointment upon the head that ran down upon the beard even Aaron's beard: that went down to the skirts of his garments" (Psalms 133:1–2).

Unity in the faith is power to the believer. Has the church lost its focus on the mission or purpose? Remember it's all about Jesus, not theology. Knowing him personally is objective number one, wouldn't you agree?

How can we accomplish this overwhelming task of restoration? Restoration can occur simply by reintroducing the Holy Spirit and his voice of revelation to the believer once again. Who can know Jesus apart from Holy Spirit revelation?

"Wherefore I give you to understand, that no man speaking by the Spirit of God calleth Jesus accursed: and that no man can say that Jesus is the Lord, but by the Holy Ghost" (1 Corinthians 12:3).

To coin the phrase of an unknown author, the

reality of failure or success is found in "when you fail to plan, you plan to fail." We need to return to the drawing board of sound doctrine. The Word of God is his plan for man, but if we fail to implement his plan for our lives, it will surely mean we plan to fail in spirit.

The restoration of unity will be the key to victory. We as Christians must look to the future survival of the church by taking part in the restoration of that which Joel the Prophet spoke, the pouring out of the Holy Spirit upon all believers' flesh. Being led of the Holy Spirit produces holy sons of God.

"For as many as are led by the Spirit of God, they are the sons of God" (Romans 8:14).

"This I say then, Walk in the Spirit, and ye shall not fulfill the lust of the flesh" (Galatians 5:16).

2. What principles have you put in place in your church for being a successful healing and restoring church?

The future of the church lay in the hands of Holy Ghost, fired-up preachers led of the Holy Spirit. This is a vital part in the restoration of the church.

"Then the twelve called the multitude of the disciples unto them, and said it is not reason that we should leave the word of God, and serve tables. Wherefore, brethren, look ye out among you seven men of honest report, full of the Holy Ghost and wisdom, whom we may appoint over this business" (Acts 6:2–3).

"And they went forth, and preached everywhere,

the Lord working with them, and confirming the Word with signs following. Amen" (Mark 16:20).

3. What advice could you offer to a new pastor beginning a new work in the area of healing and restoration?

A stern warning of advice to anyone who feels the call of God upon his or her life to serve in the ministry of his Word is this: Seek the anointing in prayer, think twice before you speak, and be sure to get the mind of Christ first before you begin to speak, and you will find success in God. Success in God is when you hear the words, "Well done, good and faithful servant."

Restoration is simply coming back to the basics and then become doers not hearers only. Spiritual laziness will never mix anymore than oil and water can mix. Through the process of homogenization, oil and water can be mixed for a brief time but will revert back to their normal state if left alone.

—Evangelist/Teacher
Dr. Dick Reuben
www.dickreuben.org

Biography
George Shafer

George Shafer was born in Dayton, Kentucky. He enrolled at a very early age at Biola College in La Mirada, California, while accepting a position as children's pastor at the Southern Baptist church in Huntington Beach, California, where he was ordained. He and Brenda received the baptism in the Holy Spirit in their home in 1970.

In 1976, he moved to Florence, Kentucky. From 1976 to 1981, he was founder of the first Jesus Coffee House Ministry and the founder of the first Christian Supper Club in the tri-state area and was co-founder of the first Christian television station in the tri-state area. He built the Isaiah House for troubled and abused children and pastored and founded a nondenominational church in Florence, Kentucky. George and Brenda co-hosted a TV talk show called the *TFJ Club* in Louisville, Kentucky, with Ed Boles.

1981–2004, Tulsa, Oklahoma

George and Brenda were co-founders of South Water Home for Girls, a home for domestically and sexually abused girls. In 1989, George and Brenda founded a nondenominational church, Midwest Agape Chapel. They also founded Pleasant Valley Youth Ranch, a lovely 230-acre ranch for domestically and sexually abused boys. In 1991, George and several church members built two churches and an orphanage in Port-au-Prince, Haiti. Pastor Shafer and his wife still pastor Midwest Agape Chapel on a lovely twenty-acre campus.

Pastor Shafer continues to travel to Africa and does seminars in Nigeria on Jewish heritage. Pastor Shafer's heritage is German Jew.

Pastor Shafer had the following to share:

> Greetings, my sister,
>
> I am sorry for just now getting back to you. I needed to pray and think this thing through, and

I have done that, so now I am attempting to respond to your three (3) questions.

Question number 1, you are asking "What is your perspective of the condition of the body of Christ today in terms of being a healing and restoring body?"

I do not believe that we are doing a very good job in healing the broken hearts of people, including God's people and the people of the world. I believe restoring the brokenhearted as stated in Isaiah 61. And I believe that we are doing a very poor job as a body of Christ in doing that as a whole. I know that there are some local churches that are doing a great job. But I believe as a whole, as a body of Christ, I think we are doing a very poor job explaining the healing virtue that Jesus has provided from Calvary.

In question number 2, you ask, "What key principles have you put in place in your church for being a successful healing and restoring church?"

Here at Midwest Agape Chapel, our vision is Isaiah 61, and how we do this is by feeding the poor, trying to clothe the naked to the best of our ability; however, we are not doing a good job of that right now physically. We are bringing restoration to the hearts of God's people. We have a youth ranch that we are getting back into full operation again to literally take children off the streets where we can begin to speak into their little lives and hearts; we call it a haven of rest, and the name of it is Pleasant Valley Youth Ranch.

At our church, I try to teach a full balance, a full menu; I teach healing prosperity, but the main thrust of what I teach is found in Isaiah 61:1–3, "bringing healing to the brokenhearted people." Luke 4:18 is the purpose of Jesus Christ, to restore and to heal; so in doing that, we have built a school and an orphanage on the island of Jamaica and have been bringing restoration physically. In my messages, I try to preach and teach a full menu of the baptism of the Holy Spirit and not just walk around praying in tongues all the time. I try to literally say we have to literally be real people. We have to use our brains. We have to see people through the eyes of Jesus. We have to hear people's hearts through the ears of Jesus, and we have to be the hands of Jesus. If we are not willing to be the hands, the feet, the eyes and the ears, then our mission is in vain. We have no real purpose in being a part of the body of Christ. So that is why we have in big bold letters a sign that reads, "Bringing Healing to the Brokenhearted People." Yes, this is our mission.

So, in number 3, you ask me, "What advise could you offer to a new pastor beginning a new work in the area of healing and restoration?"

I am assuming that you are talking about the healing as starting from the heart out. Because that is the major problem of people as a whole, is that we have a heart condition, and we must have major heart surgery. We have to have a heart transplant and without the Lord Jesus Christ giving us a heart transplant, all of the works are in vain. Because works have to cease; we have to rest in the Lord and allow the works to become the works of the Lord. Therein lies the difference. People who are work orientated rather than walking in the Spirit orientated. I am not contradicting myself here; what I am saying is simply is that if we learn to rest in the Lord, then the works that we do will manifest out of us as in James 2:18 it says, "Show me your faith without your works, and I will show you my faith by my works." So, my position is that I would offer to a new pastor starting a new work is first and foremost to find the need in your surrounding area, in your town, and in your peoples' hearts. More than likely, you are going to find the need is dealing with a heart condition. You too are going to have a heart condition. We need a heart transplant. We have got to go back to our first love.

It is not about building church buildings or who can drive the fanciest car; it's not about how many television programs or radio programs we can put on the air; they all come after. Our focus is Matthew 6:33 in seeking the kingdom of God. We have to seek his kingdom first; he has promised to bring in everything else after that. Everything will fall in line, regardless of what it looks like; everything will absolutely fall in line.

Another word of advice to a new pastor would be to go after the people's heart with every ounce that is within you. You have to become involved. I know we are in time that people do not want to become involved, especially pastors. People do not want to get involved with each other because they do not want to get hurt. Well, I am sorry; that is a part of it. If we're going to follow the footsteps of Jesus, we have to pick up our cross and go after it and just pursue the heart. We need a heart transplant! Jesus is coming very, very soon. We have to be ready, we have to trim our wicks, and we have to go back to our first love.

Thank you for the opportunity to give you my answers to the above stated questions.

Sincerely,

—Pastor George Shafer

Biography
Rabbi Brawer
Member of Tikkun Ministries and Union of Messianic Jewish Congregations

Rabbi Ira Brawer was born in 1950 in New York and was raised in an observant Jewish home. He and his family attended an orthodox synagogue, and like most Jewish young men, he was Bar-Mitzvahed at age thirteen. After falling away from Judaism as a teenager, he found the Messiah as an adult through the ministry of Eliezer Urbach with the American Board of Missions to the Jews (now called Chosen People Ministries) in 1984. He was ordained by the Union of Messianic Jewish Congregations in 1991 after completing training in the UJMC Yeshiva

Institute. He also holds a bachelor's degree from Colorado Christian University.

In 1991, answering the call of God, Rabbi Ira and his family moved to south Florida and planted Ayts Chayim Messianic Synagogue as a witness to the Jewish communities in Broward and Palm Beach counties. His wife of twenty-one years, Gloria, and their three children, Josie, Micha, and Avi, are a big part of the congregational and ministry activities. They also have two grown children: Sammi, who is married with four children and living in Colorado, and Seth, who lives in Washington DC. You can find the family at all worship services, at dance ministry outings, and at outreach ministry activities. Rabbi Ira and Gloria welcome your family to join theirs and celebrate Shabbat, the feasts and holidays, and the presence of Yeshua in our lives every day. Their vision is to lead people into the knowledge of Yeshua as their Messiah and to help them fulfill their destiny in God. This is done through healthy, strong relationships in the context of a covenant community.

I interviewed Rabbi Brawer, a Messianic Jewish believer. He presides over a Messianic congregation in Florida. I asked him to answer the same questions I had asked of the other four ministers. This is what he had to share:

1. What is your perspective of the condition of the body of Christ today in terms of being a healing and restoring body?

From my perspective, what I understand from the church is that it has lost its mission in calling, which, according to Romans 11, salvation came to the Gentiles to make Israel jealous. Paul said the mercy that God showed the Gentiles because of Israel's disobedience was the mercy that he wanted in turn to show back to Israel, back to the Jewish people. That is the mission of the church, as I understand it, of course it is to preach the Gospel and so forth.

The church being grafted into the Jewish outgrowths was for this purpose, but the church did not do that, but did the opposite by persecuting Israel and claiming to be the new Israel, that the blessing, the anointing, and the power of God has not been in the church for eighteen hundred years. Although there have been glimpses of it, because God is merciful and because his will and his kingdom will be established.

He is establishing some segments of the church to its destiny, which is to understand that (Yeshua) Jesus is not returning until his people (because he is king of the Jews), the people that he is king over call out to him and proclaim him to be king…Until that happens, he is not going to return. Because of this, the destiny of the church is intertwined with the destiny of Israel. What the church doesn't understand because of some of the many different theologies (one in particular) is basically replacing the theology of the old Israel with "the new Israel." Everything else is that God's promises to Israel are still in effect. They are still the beloved of God for the sake of the patriarch, is still in existence, so I believe that as the church awakens, (and there are some that are awaking) to the understanding of God's calling on the church to make Israel jealous, not to replace Israel, but to come along side Israel, and that Israel is still a nation whether we are in the land or outside of the land, (that means that) every Jewish person is part of the nation of Israel; part of that chosen-ness; election of God.

Although, we still believe that salvation only comes to an individual through faith in Yeshua. He said, "Go and make disciples; teach them everything that I have commanded, and lo, I am with you always even till the end of days; teach them to obey the Commandments."

We, however, don't want to talk about commandments, because we are somehow under the Law when we do that, but Jesus had no problem teaching them to obey the commandments and that is a problem. We are not teaching people to obey the commandments. We are not even teaching that the commandments are valid for today. "Oh, that has been done away with. We are under grace now." What does this tell people? It tells people, "Oh, you can do whatever you want, and the blood of Jesus will cover your sin and you are okay. This is a distortion of the Gospel.

The Gospel is the kingdom. We submit to the rules of the kingdom. It is not a one-time event. People think it is a one-time event. It is not a one-time event. It is a daily surrender. That is why repentance and transformation are a lifestyle. Repentance is not confessing our sin. Repentance is change! Confession is the first part of repentance. This is another thing, understanding what is repentance. People think if they repent, they say they are sorry, and they cry that that is repentance.

This is not repentance. It is feeling bad about your sin, and through repentance you are changed. The first command of the gospel is to "Repent, and enter into the kingdom."

We are not understanding the true gospel, the gospel that Yeshua preached, the good news of the kingdom. The good news of the kingdom is coming into the realm of the king, where we give him the opportunity to put our lives in order, which includes healing and restoration, but if we are not being taught the nature of the gospel, that it requires surrender; that it requires repentance, then healing and restoration can't take place. What happens is people pray a prayer, but yet they hold on to the kingdom of self. They hold on to their own agendas, their own hurts, their own pains, their own right to be angry, bitter; whatever it may be, and therefore, they never experience healing and restoration, even the processes of healing and counseling fall short because the basis of understanding the kingdom is not there.

It really all goes back to the right understanding of what Yeshua preached as the good news of the kingdom and that he commanded us to preach that as well. It is good news! It is truly good news that when we submit to the realm of the king (by placing our lives in his hands, if we let him) if we surrender truly, then he does put our lives in order and brings restoration and healing to every area of our lives, whether it be physical, spiritual, whether it be our family, our children, our work situations. We give him the opportunity to put all in order, and that is what being in the kingdom is all about.

From there it spreads. It is like a mustard seed that is to spread and to grow and to go forth from us, cause our lives are put in order, and our families' lives are in order. Then it goes forth from there to the people we meet, people we touch. They see what life in the kingdom is, and they want to be part of it as well. It is not just that we preach the Gospel that we say how good Jesus is and that he will make you "healthy, wealthy, and wise," but that if you are willing to give up your life, then he gives us his life. The Gospel is to be spread through our changed lives.

2. What principles have you put in place in your church for being a successful healing and restoring church?

Well, I think it begins with understanding the vision. First, the big picture, as I said in the previous question about understanding what we are and who we are in the kingdom and that there is a bigger picture that we are called into. So now, our lives are not our own, but we have a calling in life that transcends our mundane existence of my job, my family, my processions, entertainment, whatever. All those things that make up our lives are as important as those things may be, but there is something much greater than that. There is a grand scheme of things that we are part of, which gives hope and healing to people, something more important than their own lives. This is foundational. This is the big vision, and then there is the vision of our own particular congregation set forth clearly. Being able to articulate a clear vision of why we exist as a body, therefore those that are called to be part of the body have a part in that vision.

We are all called to serve, so it is easy to teach people how to serve, but what is the motivation for them to serve? Because of this … this is what I have to do? Is it part of my religious duty, or whatever, but if they see us as part of the big picture—the vision they will do it. They understand that they are a part of this vision, whether I am the doorkeeper, or whatever, I am a part of this calling, this vision that God has placed upon this local body that creates an atmosphere of excitement and enthusiasm that transcends the mundane individual problems, struggles, and whatever may be going on.

We have a mission statement that we preach on. We have core values that are listed that are clear. How we operate. Part of those core values is integrity in relationships. That the congregation has an atmosphere of hope and healing, kind of like a "greenhouse effect" where, just by being in the community, there is a healing aspect that takes place. I am not talking of private counseling and all that. Although we have that as well, but just being in the community, in a body that is healthy, that has a purpose, that knows where it's going, that creates an atmosphere of hope and healing.

We believe in long-term covenant relationships; this is a biblical principle of the kingdom that is not taught very much because we have the idea that, "I go to a church to have my needs met, and as long as my kids are happy (because we have a great youth program, and there is great worship, teaching and all this) that my needs are being met," but that is not right. Biblically, we are joined to a body. We are called to a particular body.

Now for us it is kind of easy because we are Messianic Jewish, and there is a very particular vision. You know, if you are called to it or not so in some ways there is an advantage in that, because we are not your "normal" church. Yet, we still have people coming through our doors for the wrong reasons. Well, they like the idea of being in a Jewish congregation, or they like Jewish worship or such things, whatever. Generally, those people do not stay around very long. Why? That is not what it is. I mean, it is part of it, but that is mostly what you see on the surface, but there is more to it. It is commitment.

We teach covenant relationships, so when a person comes into our body, he/she does not join a body, but is joined to the body. We teach that it is a serious commitment. Now, God moves people on (to another place) but generally, people say, "God is calling me to go someplace else," but it is a way of saying, "I have been offended, and I don't want to deal with my issues here, so I am going someplace else." There is no way to avoid that, but I think it could be minimized through teaching at the front door the model—covenant relationships. We stay together no matter what, until such a time, that it is clear to send him/her out like it says in Acts 13. They are prepared. The call of God is on their life, then everyone recognizes it, and there is a corporate. Amen.

There is a laying on of hands, and God is clearly calling this person to start a new work, to extend the kingdom. So moving out of the body is clearly for kingdom purposes. It is not based on who you know or how you feel. Now, is our congregation at a hundred percent? No, it clearly is not. I do not want to give the impression that we have the perfect congregation, but I think that it is a key principle that cerates an atmosphere for healing and restoration.

Another thing is that we acknowledge and understand that people coming in (through our doors) need ministering particularly for unbelievers. They are not coming in all cleaned up. They are coming in hurting. So, what I like to say is that we are not a hospital, but we have a hospital. If you (your church) are a hospital, then it is (full of) all sick people. Nobody wants to be in a hospital full of sick people, so we have a hospital that if you need help, we get you cleaned up and healed so that you can function in the body. If the congregation is a hospital, then everyone is sick; then no one is getting healed and there are some places like that. Their focus is on (my) hurts, (my) needs. We do not want that to be the main focus, but (instead) it is a place that you can get healing, if you need it... We all need it from the head all the way down.

We believe, my wife and I and those who are in leadership in the congregation, that the congregation should be transparent, so we need to admit (not necessarily air) everything out publicly. There are boundaries that are needed, so that people know that we are transparent, that we have issues that we have to deal with. We have kids that are not perfect and etc. I think that when we are not transparent, it creates a false pressure on the kids and family that they need to be perfect. It is very difficult for the people in the congregation then to relate to them. (They say to themselves), "Well, he is the pastor or the rabbi and so he hasn't experienced the kind of things we are experiencing." That's not true! We do! I think transparency is another key principle in leadership.

Transparency is also the key for keeping your congregation from making a god out of you. This also promotes accountability from the top down, so I have men that I am in relationship with through our network that I am accountable to... but it is through relationships, not a "from the top down bureaucratic" thing. These are men that I am in covenant with, who I have come to know over the years, that I have chosen to be affiliated with; a network of congregations that has an apostolic (and yes, sometimes this has a bad connotation to it) because it implies an autocratic type of government. It is really apostolic in simply having a pastor for a pastor, in my case a rabbi for a rabbi. Therefore, the people in the congregation know that I am submitted to someone outside of the congregation, they have a sense of security that number one, their rabbi, their leader, is not a loose cannon, and it gives me the credibility to teach about submission because I am under submission. In the right order, this gives the people a great sense of security, which contributes to healing and restoration because they feel they are not going to be abused. There is a court of appeals, so to speak…(My higher ups)…They are introduced to them. They see them. I can say here is my rabbi. This is whom I go to when I need to be corrected; he has permission to speak into my life.

We try to create a similar atmosphere for the congregation for those who want it. It is not forced on anyone, but there is an atmosphere where people can have personal accountability if they want it, where they can choose to have somebody minister to them, more one-on-one discipleship, mentoring, whatever you want to call it, which includes personal accountability and ministry accountability. Accountability is a very important principle.

Another principle is the idea of community, (as stated before), and family orientation which is a very Jewish concept. In Jewish prayers, for example, (they are always spoken in terms of) "us," such as "our Father," "we come before you." "We bow the knee before you." It is always in the form of "us," a community. It is really reflective of not just the community present, but reflective of the whole community of Israel, that we format and that we are a microcosm of it.

My experience in the church world is that the songs that we sing say, "This is my Jesus." It's "my relationship," it's "I am salvation." It is more. There in itself lies a big problem because of the self-centeredness of the Western gospel. It is self-focused, whereas biblically, Jewish understanding is community. It is a corporate focus, a corporate destiny and that is lost in the church, because the emphasis is on the individual.

3. What advice could you offer to a new pastor beginning a new work in the area of healing and restoration?

The first thing I would say to him is to focus him and his family (because if we are going to focus on this area) then we ourselves need to get as much healing and restoration as we can. Everyone is at different levels on that, but for a new minister in this area, this would be the first thing I would attend to.

Then I would recommend that he find (if he's like an independent pastor who is without a network) an older pastor, and I would offer myself (if I could help) to mentor him into this... I would tell him to concentrate more in the area of accountability, so that he could lay a foundation for the ministry of transparency, starting with himself, because (in the church) there has to be an atmosphere that people can come into (the congregation) where they feel safe.

People are not going to feel safe if there is this image of perfection or an image where the pastor is above everything. There has to be a certain level of transparency at the top. In order to do that, you have to be secure with whom you are. You have to have healing, have accountability, and be willing to submit (on an on going basis) to someone who is older in the ministry, a place where you can get a reality reading, reality check from time to time; a person to run things by and get input. This is really what it is. It is getting input before you make decisions. It should be someone who can tell you that you are off base or you are going to get in trouble if you do that. This is what I have with my mentor. He is someone I can call and run things by. When I haven't done that at times, I have paid the price. So I have learned from experience that this is a safety (net), and this is how God sets us up. To me this is a major part of what God calls order, God's government.

God is a God of order, and the government is on his shoulders. He wants us to operate in order and with proper government. This simply means we have people that we can look to, to get input, get counsel. There is a safety mode to counsel. It also should be directed. In other words, we should be getting counsel from the people that we respect, who know us, love us, and are concerned about us.

I know people that ask a lot of people for advice. Then they do what they want to do. They are not submitted. They say, "Well I got counseled." Then I have to say, "But you did not submit." There are others who come to counsel and inform you of their decision. For example, they say, "I am considering a job change, so I prayed about it, and I think I am supposed to do it. I told my boss, 'I'll take the job,' but I am here for counsel. Listen, I want you to pray about me taking this new job." This is not counsel or being accountable. It is really informing me of their decision. I ask, "Are you informing me of something you have already decided, or are you asking for counsel? It sounds like you already have made the decision." I can pretty much tell they have already made the decision. Some have said, "I want to marry the person." I also have actually had someone come to me and

> say, "Guess what? I'm engaged" when they are supposedly in accountability with me. Of course, we should not control whom people marry or what jobs they take or anything like that, but don't say you are in accountability and then make these decisions without getting input, because this is not accountability. You have a conscience before the Holy Spirit to make those decisions and you are not in sin, but don't call it accountability; just say we are friends or you attend here (are part of the congregation). We have to make that distinction.
>
> We have a lot of people in the congregation who are not in accountability with me, and that's okay. I can't have accountability with everyone. I can only have it with a few people, the people who are really serious and want to be discipled and want to make disciples. Accountability goes right alongside discipleship. We need to understand the difference between discipleship and counsel and teach those in our care the difference. These are key factors to becoming a minister.

From these letters and this interview, we can appreciate these pastors,' evangelists,' and rabbi's heartfelt desire to reach the hurting with the love of God. This is the heartbeat of the cause of Christ, what he displayed on the cross through his sacrifice of love, and obedience.

Let us all strive for mastery of this goal: wiping out the spot of pride and ironing out the wrinkle of no love by coming to terms with the needs that exist within the four walls and the cries of those who exist outside of them.

Closing Comments from the Author

The bride of Christ today has accomplished great feats and has overcome a great deal! She is to be commended for her commitment to the bridegroom's return. However, as with all things, there is always room for improvement, some of which have been outlined in the chapters of this book.

Let us be encouraged! And let us be as wise as the serpent! Let us awaken to the clarion call to wipe out the spot of pride and iron out the wrinkle of no love before our bridegroom arrives. We have the authority within us to promote light in the midst of the darkness of the times to expose them and render them obsolete!

Can you hear him say, "Beloved, do you love me? Are you in wait of my return?"

We are at war! But our enemy is not each other! We are a family.

We are the salt of the earth. We cannot allow ourselves to be distracted by each other. Divided, we will not stand. However, focused on peace, we can mend the fences within our churches.

> Why is this important, you might ask? Simply, because if we are not careful to do so, the darkness of this world will make it possible to cover any spot and wrinkle on our dress from the world and its stain from ourselves. Keeping us bound to continue in conditional Christian behavior that deceives us into believing, we will be allowed to enter the bridal chamber with a spotted and wrinkled dress, un-presentable to the bridegroom.

Do not be fooled! You know and I know by studying his Word that many will hear on the day of judgment, "Depart from me; I never knew you!" However, today we still have the power and the time to address any blemishes on our dress and correct them. We have the power within us to do what is necessary to prepare for our precious bridegroom! May he be glorified in our efforts and in our time of waiting.

> Awake! Awake! Can you hear the cry from those who have overcome adversity ringing in your ear? I can!

You and I have the tools to evaluate the condition of our dress garment.

Today, ask him to reveal her condition to you. Ask him to expose whatever is not pleasing to him; believe that he will, and he will! We can prepare and make ourselves presentable to our bridegroom, spot free and wrinkle free, if we take a moment to step into the light before our Father and allow his light to expose any blemishes that may exist on our dress.

Today, take ownership of his compassion, humility, and above all, his unconditional love for others and yourself.

1. Make a sincere attempt to arm yourself with the tools available in his Word to help you.
2. Refrain from the lure of contemporary theology as a source for bridging the religious generational gap.
3. Define sin and its effects, both spiritually and emotionally.
4. Address sin from a convicting standpoint, not from a condemning point of view from our pulpits.
5. Be examples in our struggles, exposing sin and dealing with sin by God's standards.
6. Identify with whose you are; embrace your bridal status
7. Reacquaint yourself with his righteousness and its benefits
8. Forego Christian conditional behavior and embrace instead God's unconditional Christian behavior found in his traits and character.

9. Take ownership of his promises.
10. Embrace his blessings.
11. Take ownership of his gifts, the fruits of the spirit (Galatians 5:22–23), and the gifts of the Spirit (1 Corinthians 12 and 14).
12. Implement conflict management through peaceful alternatives.
13. Stand guard in your church against the spirit of Jezebel.
14. Stay focused on his statutes and commandments as your guide.
15. Guard ourselves against the spot of pride and the wrinkle of no love by submitting to him with a penitent heart for sin in repentance.
16. Worship him often, which acts as a repellent against pride!
17. Above all, never forget our highest call to Christendom, lifting up the name of Jesus in all and through all. For in doing so, we bring him honor, not shame caused by inconsistency, in our commitment as his bride to be.

Let us always remember that he reciprocates our gallant actions performed toward others with victory and honor as his bride, thereby affording us an eternal life of peace, joy, love, and liberty in his everlasting loving arms.

My desire is that you have come away from reading this project with a sense of urgency and a sense of empowerment to carry on in your mission to fulfilling his call in your life. May you find yourself in the center of his will for your life and fulfill your purpose and destiny. May it be pleasing to him, for he has chosen you to accomplish his tasks and do his bidding.

Praise always his precious name, Jesus Christ, the lover of your soul.

Books and Booklets By Dr. Marilyn Salmonson Available!

Voice of Encouraging Thoughts - Devotional

It is a Monday – Friday devotional!

It contains over 450 Scripture verses!

The Index covers over 140 subjects!

Fasting As Unto the Lord

Learn how to Fast!

What is a Fast?

The Benefits of a Fast!

What is not a Fast?

What Are You Struggling With? Booklet Series

Overcome Struggles with:

Self-Esteem

Fear

Unforgiveness

Unbelief

For Information on More Titles Available Visit:

www.encouragingthoughts.org

Endnotes

1. *What The Bible Is All About?* by Henrietta C. Mears, page 465
2. *Tyndale New Testament Commentaries: Romans* by F. F. Bruce, pages 94,
3. *Word Meanings in the New Testament* by Ralph Earl, page 136.
4. *Vines Expository Dictionary of Old and New Testament Words* by W. E. Vine, page 2
5. *The New Shorter Oxford Dictionary* by Oxford Press, page 2600.
6. *Experiencing God* by Henry T. Blackaby and Claude V. King, page 271.
7. *Holy Bible: The New King James Version* by Thomas Nelson Publishers.

8. *Halley's Bible Handbook* by Zondervan Publishing House, pages 588 and 5

9. *New Bible Commentary* edited by G. J. Wenham, J. A. Motyer, D. A. Carson, R. T. France 21st edition, pages 1239 and 1240.

10. *What the Bible Is All About* by Henrietta C. Mears, page 463.

11. *The Oxford Bible Commentary* edited by John Barton and John Muddiman, page 1092.

12. *The New Unger's Bible Handbook* by Merrill F. Unger, page 250.

13. *The Gifts and Ministries of the Holy Spirit* by Lester Sumrall.

14. *Fasting As Unto the Lord* by Marilyn Salmonson, page 103.

15. *Dictionary.com Unabridged (v 1.1): Based on the Random House Unabridged Dictionary, © Random House, Inc. 2006.*

16. *Churches That Heal* by Doug Murren—Found in foreword by George Barna, pages ix–x.

17. *Churches That Heal* by Doug Murren, pages 34–35.

18. *Dictionary.com Unabridged (v 1.1): Based on the Random House Unabridged Dictionary, © Random House, Inc. 2006.*

19. *Churches That Heal* by Doug Murren, page 217.

20. *Churches That Heal* by Doug Murren, pages 217- 218.

21. *The New Shorter Oxford English Dictionary* edited by Lesley Brown, page 476.

22. *The Peace Makers* by Ken Sande, page 25.

23. Ibid, page 76.

24. *The Peace Makers* by Ken Sande, page 77.

25. Ibid, page 79.

26. *The Peace Makers* by Ken Sande page 9.

27. *The Peace Makers* by Ken Sande, page 13.

28. *The Peace Makers* by Ken Sande, pages 102 and 103.

29. *The Peace Makers* by Ken Sande, pages 10 and 11.

30. *The Peace Makers* by Ken Sande, pages 146, 149, and 156.

31. *The Peace Makers* by Ken Sande, page 40.

32. *3,4508 Bible People & Places* by Inspirational Press New York, page 191.

33. *The Jezebel Spirit* by Francis Frangipane, page 8.

34. *3,458 Bible People & Places* by Inspirational Press, New York, page 191.

35. Ibid, page 191.

36. *The Jezebel Spirit: Discernment Series* by Francis Frangipane, page 9.

37. *A Survey of the New Testament* by Robert H. Gundry, page 25.

38. *Unmasking the Jezebel Spirit* (previously titled *The Veiled Ploy*) by John Paul Jackson, page 66.
39. *The Jezebel Spirit: Discernment Series* by Francis Frangipane, page 14.
40. *Unmasking the Jezebel Spirit* (previously titled *The Veiled Ploy*) by John Paul Jackson, page 66.
41. *Unmasking the Jezebel Spirit* (previously titled *The Veiled Ploy*) by John Paul Jackson, page 66.
42. *The Jezebel Spirit: Discernment Series* by Francis Frangipane, page 33.

Bibliography

Barton, J., Muddiman, J. Ed. *The Oxford Bible Commentary*. New York: Oxford University Press, 2001.

Blackaby, Henry T., King, Claude V. *Experiencing God*. Tennessee: Broadman & Holman Publishers, 1994, 1998.

Brown, Lesley edited. *The New Shorter Oxford English Dictionary on Historical Principles*, New York: Oxford University Press, 1973, 1993.

Bruce, F. Frank. *The Tyndale New Testament Commentaries*: Rev. ed. of: The Epistle of Paul to the Romans. England: Inter-Varsity Press, 1963. Reprint, Michigan: Wm. B. Eerdmans Publishing, 2002.

Carson, D.A., France, R. T., Motyer, J. A., Wenham, G. J. ed. *The New Bible Commentary*. England: Inter-Varsity Press 1953, 1954, 1970. Reprint, Illinois: Intervarsity Press, 1994.

Davis, E.g., Lola., *Toward a World Religion for a New Age*, New York: Coleman Publishing, 1983.

Dictionary.com Unabridged (v 1.1): Based on the Random House Unabridged Dictionary, © Random House, Inc. 2006.

Earl, Ralph. *Word Meanings in the New Testament*: One volume ed. Missouri: Beacon Hill Press, 1986. Reprint, Missouri: Baker Book House, 1994.

Easton, M. G. *Easton's 1897 Bible Dictionary*, and 3rd ed., Arizona: Thomas Nelson Publishers, 1897.

Frangipane, Francis. *Discernment Series: The Jezebel Spirit*, Iowa: Arrow Publications, 1991.

Gundry, Robert H. *A Survey of the New Testament*, 3rd ed., Michigan: Zondervan Publishing House, 1994.

Halley's Bible Handbook. 24th ed., Michigan: Zondervan Publishing House, 1962, 1965.

Holy Bible, New King James Version. Tennessee, Canada, New York: Thomas Nelson Publishers, 1982.

Houghton, Co. *Dictionary of the English Language*, 4th ed., Massachusetts: Houghton Miffin Co., 2000.

Jackson, John P. *Unmasking the Jezebel Spirit* (previously titled *The Veiled Ploy*), New Hampshire: Streams Publications, 2002.

Mears, Henrietta C. *What the Bible Is All About*, 2nd Rev. ed. California: Regal Books, 1997.

Murren, Doug. *Churches That Heal*, Louisiana: Howard Publishing Co., Inc., 1999.

Nelson, Thomas. Inc., *3,458 Bible People & Places*, New York: Inspirational Press, 1993.

Ostling, Richard N. 'Power, Glory—and Politics,' New York: Time Magazine, Feb. Issue, 1986.

Sande, Ken. *Peacemaker*, 2nd Rev ed., Michigan: Baker Books House, 1997.

Salmonson, Marilyn. *Fasting As Unto the Lord,* 2nd ed., Pennsylvania: Whitaker House Publishing, 2000, 2003.

The Amplified Bible. Michigan: The Lockman Foundation and Zondervan Publishing house, [1958].

The New Shorter Oxford English Dictionary. New York: Oxford University Press, [1973, 1993].

Unger, Merrill F. *The New Unger's Bible Handbook*. Chicago: Moody Press, 1998.

Vine, W. E. *Vines Expository Dictionary of Old and New Testament Words.*, London: Oliphants Ltd., 1949. Reprint, Michigan: Baker Book House, 1978.